L I F E W A Y S

The Shawnee

R A Y M O N D   B I A L

BENCHMARK BOOKS

MARSHALL CAVENDISH
NEW YORK

SERIES CONSULTANT: JOHN BIERHORST

ACKNOWLEDGMENTS

This book would not have been possible without the kind assistance of several individuals and organizations. I would like to thank everyone at Zane Shawnee Caverns near Bellefontaine, Ohio, and the Eastern Shawnee Tribe of Oklahoma who generously shared information and permitted me to make photographs. My travels to Ohio and Oklahoma were a truly memorable and enjoyable experience.

I would like to express my deepest appreciation to my editor Christina Gardeski for her attentive review of this manuscript. I am again indebted to John Bierhorst for his thorough review of my efforts. As always, I would like to thank my wife Linda and my children Anna, Sarah, and Luke for their consistent support of my work.

Benchmark Books
Marshall Cavendish
99 White Plains Road
Tarrytown, New York 10591-9001
www.marshallcavendish.com
Text copyright © 2004 by Raymond Bial
Map copyright © 2004 by Marshall Cavendish Corporation
Map by Rodica Prato

Library of Congress Cataloging-in-Publication Data
Bial, Raymond.
The Shawnee / by Raymond Bial.
p. cm.—(Lifeways)
Summary: Discusses the history, culture, beliefs, changing ways, and notable people of the Shawnee.
Includes bibliographical references and index.
ISBN 0-7614-1682-X
1. Shawnee Indians—History—Juvenile literature. 2. Shawnee Indians—Social life and customs—Juvenile literature. [1. Shawnee Indians. 2. Indians of North America—East (U.S.)] I. Title.
II. Series: Bial, Raymond. Lifeways.
E99.S35B53 2003
974.004'973—dc21
2003001447

Printed in Italy
6 5 4 3 2 1

Photo Research by Anne Burns Images

Cover Photos by Raymond Bial

The photographs in this book are used with permission and through the courtesy of: *Ray Bial*: pp. 1, 6, 8 ,9, 14, 18, 25, 28, 30, 31, 33, 34, 40, 41, 43, 49, 51, 53, 55, 56, 57, 58, 59, 60, 68, 74, 75, 78, 80, 87, 88, 89, 90, 91, 94, 96, 98, 100, 101. *Art Resource*: p. 16 *The New York Public Library. North Wind Pictures*: p. 21. *Western History Collection, University of Oklahoma Libraries*: pp. 38, 45, 93, 105. *Museum of American Indian/Smithsonian Institution*: p. 63. *Corbis*: p. 82 *Bettman. Ohio Historical Society*: pp. 106, 109. *Granger Collection*: pp. 113, 115.

This book is dedicated to the Shawnee
in Ohio, Oklahoma, and other states
who have long struggled
to find a home for themselves
and their children.

Contents

Author's Note

AT THE DAWN OF THE TWENTIETH CENTURY, NATIVE Americans were thought to be a vanishing race. However, despite four hundred years of warfare, deprivation, and disease, American Indians have not gone away. Countless thousands have lost their lives, but over the course of this century the populations of native tribes have grown tremendously. Even as American Indians struggle to adapt to modern Western life, they have also kept the flame of their traditions alive—the language, religion, stories, and the everyday ways of life. An exhilarating renaissance in Native American culture is now sweeping the nation from coast to coast.

The Lifeways books depict the social and cultural life of the major nations, from the early history of native peoples in North America to their present-day struggles for survival and dignity. Historical and contemporary photographs of traditional subjects, as well as period illustrations, are blended throughout each book so that readers may gain a sense of family life in a tipi, a hogan, or a longhouse.

No single book can comprehensively portray the intricate and varied lifeways of an entire tribe, or nation. I only hope that young people will come away with a deeper appreciation for the rich tapestry of Indian culture—both then and now—and a keen desire to learn more about these first Americans.

1. Origins

The Shawnee lived in scattered
bands along the streams and rivers
in the forests of eastern North America.

FOR COUNTLESS GENERATIONS, THE SHAWNEE (SHAW-NEE) MADE THEIR way along the woodland paths and waterways of eastern North America. Hunters and farmers, they traveled in scattered bands, settled for a while along a river or stream, and then moved on. They allied with some tribes and battled others. By the 1600s, they were trading and waging war with the French and the English. By the late 1700s, they were vigorously resisting those American settlers who dared venture west of the Appalachian Mountains. They were also struggling to preserve their way of life. They recalled their history and traditions in stories told in the evenings around the flickering light of the fire. Here is one story that recounts how Our Grandmother created the world and the people who lived there:

Our Grandmother

The world was created by Our Grandmother. We sometimes call her Cloud. In the beginning, when there was nothing, she came down from above and made a turtle. Our Grandmother next created the earth, which was supported on the back of the turtle.

Our Grandmother shaped the earth into mountains. She created forests and prairies. She also made rivers, lakes, and marshes. Animals and people came to live on the newly formed land. During this time, Our Grandmother lived on the earth with her grandson, who was called Rounded-Side or Cloudy Boy, and a small dog.

Our Grandmother encouraged Rounded-Side to be well-behaved. "Don't do this, and don't do that," she told him.

But the little boy always wondered, "Why does she have these rules?"

Despite his grandmother's instructions, Rounded-Side did whatever he wanted. One day, he ran away to a forbidden place where he encountered a fish monster with a huge stomach. Rounded-Side went home, but he was curious about the fish. So, the next day he decided to return to the strange place. When he arrived, he rushed over and stuck a knife in the stomach of the fish monster.

Water gushed from the cut and the boy ran for his life. With the water rushing after him, he raced home to his grandmother. Together, they jumped into a boat and escaped the flood. However, all the people drowned.

Gazing upon the floodwaters, Our Grandmother did not know what to do. She called upon Crawfish and asked him to plunge into the depths of the water and bring back a little mud. He did as she asked, and Our Grandmother took the mud from his pinchers. Crawfish dove into the water again and again, returning with some mud each time.

Our Grandmother then called upon Buzzard. "You must dry this mud," she told him. So, Buzzard rubbed the mud on his wings and flew away. As he flew, air flowed over his wings and dried the mud.

When the flood waters receded, there was the earth again. But the ancient people had all died. So, Our Grandmother created new people. She did not make the Shawnee first but began with a Delaware man and woman. She placed them on the east side of a fire she had kindled. Then she created one group, or division, of the

Shawnee in the form of an old man and woman. She next created a young couple whose children would eventually form the other Shawnee divisions.

After she had made these people, Our Grandmother and Rounded-Side went back to their home in the sky. But the boy told her, "I want to go back and hunt deer."

Instantly suspicious, Our Grandmother cautioned him, "Do not tease that young couple."

But the boy went immediately to the couple and made fun of the young man and woman for not being able to have children. They had been infertile for two years, because Our Grandmother had not made them properly. But she corrected her blunder, and the couple had twin boys who started the other divisions of the Shawnee.

Our Grandmother did not object when Rounded-Side wanted to create all the other native tribes so that the Shawnee would have plenty of friends and enemies.

Once all the people were created, Our Grandmother showed them how to hunt game and gather plants for food and medicine. She taught them to grow corn and other crops. She taught them to build houses and gave them laws so they could govern themselves.

With the help of her grandson and the spirits known as the Thunderbirds, Our Grandmother gave sacred packs to the people. She taught them ceremonial dances and other religious practices. Because of Our Grandmother and Rounded-Side, the Shawnee have been able to prosper for many generations.

Early History

Never united as a single tribe, the loosely organized Shawnee were composed of various groups, usually referred to as divisions. In these scattered bands, they ranged as far east as the Susquehanna Valley in Pennsylvania, and as far south as Alabama. At times, they roved as far west as the Mississippi River and as far north as the Great Lakes. They were a mysterious people, because they moved so often and ranged so widely—certainly more so than the other tribes that lived east of the Mississippi River.

The Shawnee usually traveled to a new area, established a village, and lived there for a few months or sometimes for as long as a few years. Renowned as warriors, they were often invited to settle with other tribes with which they were allied. In exchange for helping to defend a village they received a share of their allies' harvest and hunting. The Shawnee traded with the tribes found throughout their extensive territory. They exchanged pottery, corn, and other foods for minerals and feathers. The Shawnee also raided enemy camps and villages for booty and hostages. Whether to hunt, wage war, or trade, they traveled mostly on foot along the well-worn trails through the woods. They also traveled along the rivers in dugout canoes.

According to tradition, the Shawnee were once allied with the Lenape (later known as the Delaware) and the Nanticoke and lived as far north as Labrador in Newfoundland. Rather, they probably originated in or just north of the Ohio River valley from an early native culture known as the Fort Ancient. The Shawnee may also

*T*rees towered in the dense forests of Shawnee territory in what are now the states of Pennsylvania and Ohio.

have originated in southeastern North America. The English word "Shawnee" comes from the Shawnee's own name for themselves, *shawanwa*, which means "person of the south" or "southerner." Yet, because they ranged so widely and mingled with other tribes, their ancestry remains a mystery. As they wandered through various regions, they became acquainted with the other tribes from whom they adopted beliefs and customs. The Shawnee are thought to have acquired certain important rituals from the Sauk, Fox, and Kickapoo who lived in the present-day Midwest. They shared many customs with the Illinois and the Miami tribes. Their villages and complex political organization were similar to those of the Cherokee and the other southeastern tribes, and the Illinois and the Miami. Shawnee bands often formed alliances with the Huron, Erie, Delaware, and Susquehannock to battle their fiercest enemies, the five tribes of the Iroquois Confederacy. Some Shawnee groups lived in the south among the Creek who had long been their friends.

The Shawnee may have first encountered Europeans in 1539 or 1540, when the Spanish expedition led by Hernando de Soto explored the southeastern part of the continent. Over the next hundred years, it is likely that the Shawnee occasionally encountered the French, who were establishing colonies in Canada and venturing into the Great Lakes region. The next recorded contact was around 1660, when French trappers and traders reached the present-day states of Tennessee and South Carolina. No one is certain of the precise date, because these accounts were written by captives or lone individuals in the wilderness. In 1662, Jerome Lalemant described the

*T*he Shawnee may have first encountered Europeans when Spanish explorer
Hernando de Soto journeyed through the Southeast.

Shawnee as living along a beautiful river to the southwest of the Iroquois. In 1669, the Shawnee were found living above the Falls of the Ohio, across the river from the present-day site of Louisville, Kentucky. In 1670, Jacques Marquette noted that the Shawnee lived to the southeast of the Illinois tribes, a reference most likely to the Peoria. The Shawnee probably also came into contact with the French when explorer René-Robert Cavelier de La Salle explored the Great Lakes and the Mississippi River. In 1673, Marquette wrote that the Ohio River flowed "from the lands of the East, where dwell the people called Chaouanons [Shawnee] in so great numbers that in one district there are as many as twenty-three villages, and fifteen in another, quite near one another."

The Shawnee's most complex and hostile relationship was with the five tribes of the Iroquois Confederacy—the Cayuga, Mohawk, Oneida, Onondaga, and Seneca. Large numbers of Shawnee did not move into Pennsylvania until they were assured that hostilities had ended. However, the Iroquois most likely only made peace after they came to view the Shawnee, like the Delaware, as subordinate to their power. As the Shawnee moved west, the Iroquois lost some control over them. In western Pennsylvania and Ohio, the Shawnee allied with the Seneca, although they were one of the tribes of the Iroquois Confederacy. The two tribes later moved together to Indian Territory.

As early as the sixteenth century, the Iroquois may have begun pushing scattered bands of Shawnee into Ohio, and continued to frequently wage war against them. Between 1662 and 1673, in particular, the Iroquois repeatedly attacked the Shawnee. The Shawnee

*T*he Shawnee established their villages along the rivers that branched throughout their extensive territory.

broke into a number of groups that scattered throughout the region. Many people settled on the northern banks of the Ohio River. Some bands drifted southeast and around 1674 settled on the Savannah River in South Carolina. In 1683, several hundred Shawnee migrated to the fort that La Salle had established at Starved Rock in Illinois. They remained there until around 1688. Around 1692, a band of 172 Shawnee, probably from Starved Rock, moved near the mouth of the Susquehanna River in Maryland. In 1694, another group moved from the Ohio River valley into eastern Pennsylvania. In the early eighteenth century, the Maryland band moved up the Susquehanna River into Pennsylvania, to establish an important settlement among the Delaware and Susquehannock. Many of those living on the Savannah River joined the Shawnee in Pennsylvania. Here, they often shared the same settlements with the Delaware and later moved together into the Ohio River valley. In the early nineteenth century, the Shawnee and the Delaware relocated together across the Mississippi River.

After 1715, some Shawnee groups in the southern region moved to the Chattahoochee River in northern Georgia where they joined several Muscogee (Upper Creek) towns. Although the Shawnee often warred with the southeastern tribes, especially the Chickasaw and Catawba, they maintained ancient alliances with the bands of the Creek confederacy. Although by the early 1700's most of the Shawnee were concentrated in other regions, the towns in the Creek confederacy usually included at least one group of Shawnee. In the nineteenth century, the Shawnee also established close ties with the Cherokee, and a large group of Shawnee eventually joined the Cherokee Nation.

The Shawnee living in eastern Pennsylvania established ties with the English colonists. They came to depend on the European trade goods and rum they obtained from the British in exchange for hides and furs. Many Shawnee succumbed to alcohol and became indebted to the traders. Since the Shawnee needed large expanses of wilderness for hunting and to maintain their way of life, they were especially threatened by the westward push of English settlers. By 1720, as game became scarce and the land was sold to English colonists by the Delaware and Iroquois, the Shawnee were again moving westward. The ongoing conflict with the Iroquois also prompted them to move west.

In 1731, about 1,400 Shawnee lived in western Pennsylvania. Around 1739, some of these Shawnee fled down the Ohio River and established a settlement known later as Lower Shawnee Town, on the Ohio near the mouth of the Scioto River. Meanwhile, other Shawnee groups were migrating westward, primarily to escape the unscrupulous English traders. Chiefs petitioned the Pennsylvania government to regulate trade and enforce laws against providing rum to the Shawnee, but these requests were ignored.

In 1745, most of the Shawnee took part in an uprising in which they pillaged the stores of several traders. They fled Pennsylvania with a half-Shawnee trader named Peter Chartier and went to Lower Shawnee Town. Others went to northern Kentucky and settled a new village. Later, they abandoned this village and moved south. There they clashed with the Chickasaw and settled among the Creek. After 1752, many Shawnee returned to Lower Shawnee Town and it became a tribal center. Other Shawnee had moved to the Cumberland River, near the present site of Nashville. In 1756, the Chickasaw drove them away and they moved to a new home on the lower Ohio River.

*S*hawnee warriors helped to defeat British general Edward Braddock on his march to Fort Duquesne in the French and Indian Wars.

English traders briefly regained the trust of the Shawnee in Ohio, but they could not protect them against the French. In part for self-defense, the Shawnee sided with the French as the French and Indian Wars raged in North America. In 1755, Shawnee warriors played a major role in the ambush and defeat of British general Edward Braddock in a surprise attack east of Pittsburgh. After this victory, they terrorized the English settlements on the frontier, in what is now West Virginia, western Maryland, and Pennsylvania. Conflicts persisted until the British took Fort Duquesne at Pittsburgh, which the retreating French had burned, established Fort Pitt in its place, and restored their control of the region.

The Shawnee in western Pennsylvania then joined the tribe living in the Scioto River valley. A few years later the Shawnee from the lower Ohio followed them. Except for those still living in Alabama, the Shawnee were again united as a tribe. When the British won the French and Indian Wars, the Shawnee came to believe that their territory in the Ohio River valley would soon be overrun by settlers. Angered over British policies and at the prospect of losing their lands, Shawnee warriors continued to attack settlements and seize captives along the frontier. Led by chiefs Hokolesqua and Puckeshinwa, most Shawnee took part in a major uprising in 1763 and 1764 that came to be known as Pontiac's Rebellion.

Although the revolt failed, the British conceded to the Royal Proclamation of 1763, an agreement in which Native Americans, including the Shawnee, were granted all the territory west of the Allegheny Mountains. The Proclamation Line of 1763 was to protect Shawnee lands from further encroachment by settlers. However, late in 1764, under the leadership of Cornstalk, the Shawnee fought the British over loss of land, and the agreement was invalidated by the Fort Stanwix Treaty of 1768. This treaty opened all the land between the Allegheny Mountains and the Ohio River to settlers. The Shawnee lost vast stretches of their hunting lands. In this treaty, Kentucky was also opened to English settlers.

Although the Shawnee did not generally live in Kentucky, the forests and fields there were an important hunting ground for them.

The Shawnee were further pressured when Virginia's colonial governor, John Murray, the Earl of Dunmore, declared that he would issue land grants on both sides of the Ohio River. The matter became a crisis in 1774 when frontiersmen murdered thirteen Shawnee and other native people in a series of unprovoked attacks. Shawnee chiefs decided not to wage war, but families of the victims avenged the deaths by killing thirteen settlers. This retaliation triggered what came to be known as Lord Dunmore's War. Lord Dunmore had claimed Kentucky and planned to settle this region. Determined to enforce his plan, he ordered a force of nine thousand militiamen to march into Shawnee territory. A smaller group embarked from Fort Pitt on the present site of Pittsburgh, and another larger force, under the command of Colonel Andrew Lewis, marched out of Fort Union in Virginia. The two forces were to unite midway in their journey, then attack the Shawnee villages. However, about sixty miles from the meeting place, a war party led by Puckeshinwa and Blue Jacket attacked Lewis and his troops. In what came to be known as the Battle of Point Pleasant, the Shawnee fought to a draw, at best, and Puckeshinwa was killed. The Shawnee finally had to accept the Ohio River as the southern boundary of their territory.

As France and Great Britain struggled for control of North America, the Shawnee had skillfully played them against each other by shifting their support from one to the other. However, the continual warfare and the European diseases, for which they had no resistance, devastated the Shawnee. At the time of first contact with Europeans there may have been between ten and twelve thousand Shawnee in eastern North America. By the time of the American Revolution their numbers had dropped to no more than three thousand people. The Shawnee found themselves divided and exhausted and their way of life changing forever as they confronted their next struggle—the union of tribes to resist the westward push of American settlers.

The People and the Land

The broad territory of the Shawnee encompassed three geographic areas: the Ohio River valley, the land east of the Allegheny Mountains, and the southern United States. These areas varied in both climate and geography. In the southern reaches, from the Carolinas and the Atlantic coast to Alabama and the Gulf of Mexico, the summers tended to be hot and humid. During the winters, there was occasional snow, but the weather tended to be relatively mild. Farther north, from Pennsylvania to Ohio, the summers might be less severe, but winters often brought intense cold and heavy snows.

The terrain varied from the ancient, worn peaks of the Appalachian Mountains to the low floodplains of the Ohio River. The mountains gave way to broad valleys, rolling hills, and sweeping prairies. There were also stretches of low ground dotted with lakes, marshes, and swamps. Throughout the region, the dense forest was a constant feature. It blanketed the land from the Atlantic Ocean almost to the Mississippi River.

*T*he forests that ranged throughout Shawnee territory provided the tribe with food, clothing, and shelter.

The forests had always been there, a vast and seemingly limitless woods alternating between broad-leafed hardwoods and stands of white pine. There were clusters of oaks and maples and patches of hemlock, beech, and basswood. Shawnee territory encompassed forests ranging from the southern hardwoods to the wilderness of spruce, fir, and pine trees at the northern reaches. As the Shawnee journeyed west, the tulip trees and hemlocks became sparse. As they traveled beneath the canopy

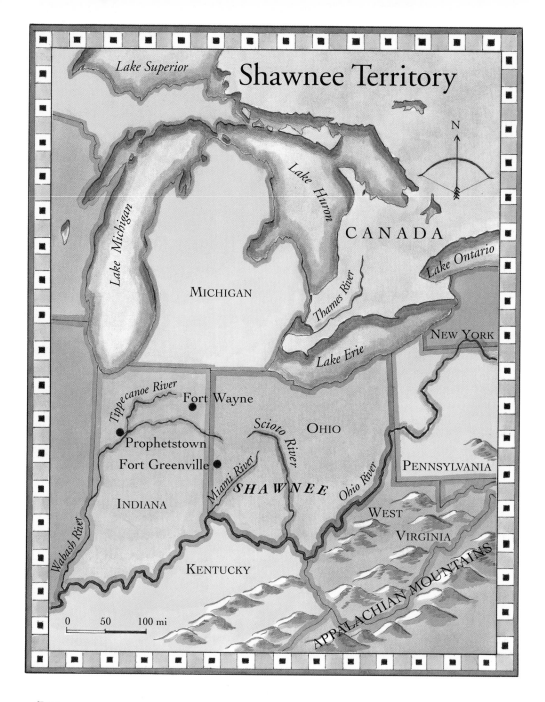

This map shows the sprawling territory of the Shawnee before they were forced to move to Indian Territory west of the Mississippi River.

of the great forests of chestnuts, oaks, and white pines, they entered forests of hard maples and beeches. In Ohio, they found occasional patches of open, grassy land and marshes, teeming with waterfowl.

As one approached the Wabash River in Indiana, the forest was broken by an occasional savannah dotted with burr oaks. Farther west, in Illinois, the land opened into sprawling prairies of big bluestem grasses, purple coneflowers, black-eyed Susans, and myriad other plants. There were no mountains here, just occasional rolling hills and stretches of land so flat that it appeared to be the floor of the sky. The prairie grasses were taller than a man, yet there were still clumps of forests rising from the seas of grass and flowers, and trees fringed the rivers and streams.

Although they sometimes hunted on the prairies, for the most part, the Shawnee knew the woods and rivers. Two great drainage systems—the Ohio River to the south and the Great Lakes to the north—converged on the Ohio country and provided a means for travel. The Shawnee and other tribes relied on the network of river highways to travel east and west, north and south, throughout the region. The land was laced with rivers, ranging from small streams to the broad, meandering Ohio River. Some of the rivers and trails led north to the Great Lakes. Others, in West Virginia and Pennsylvania, led across the Appalachian Mountains. Still others led southward into Kentucky, the Carolinas, and Alabama. The rivers branched throughout these regions—the Allegheny and Monongahela Rivers in Pennsylvania; the Muskingum, Miami, and Scioto Rivers in Ohio; the Tippecanoe and Wabash in Indiana; the Cumberland in Kentucky and Tennessee; and the Kentucky and Alabama Rivers in the states of the same names. The Shawnee often settled along the banks of these rivers, but never for long.

The woods abounded with game and the waters teemed with fish. The Shawnee gathered wild plants for food and medicine and tended corn in small clearings near their villages. They hunted deer and other animals in the woods and caught fish in the streams.

They allied with friendly tribes and fought their enemies to protect their hunting grounds. To the colonists who pushed westward, the forest was a forbidding place, although it offered plentiful game and cheap land. However, to the Shawnee, it had always been their home, a place that provided food, clothing, and shelter. For more than a century, they fought desperately to keep this land.

The traditional homeland of the Shawnee was crossed by many creeks and rivers and dotted with marshes, all teeming with wildlife.

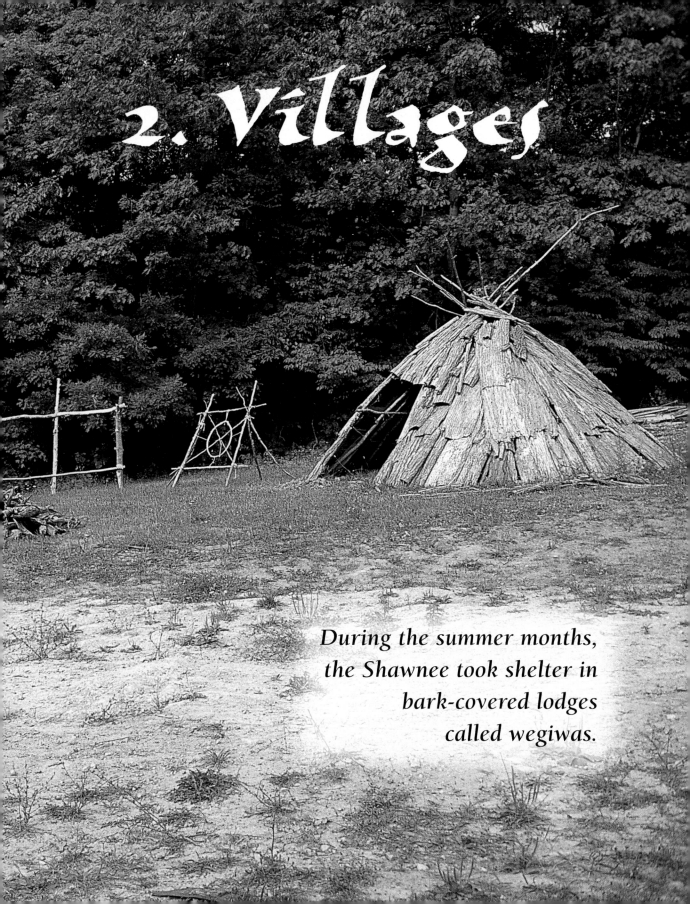

2. Villages

During the summer months,
the Shawnee took shelter in
bark-covered lodges
called wegiwas.

IN THE SUMMER, THE SHAWNEE GATHERED IN SMALL TOWNS AND villages, consisting of bark-covered lodges. Villages varied in size, depending on the time period and location of the settlement. A small community might have a cluster of lodges sheltering a few families while the largest towns had more than a hundred dwellings and over a thousand inhabitants. The village was often surrounded by a high, sturdy fence known as a palisade. Made of posts sharpened on one end and stuck vertically into the ground, and lashed together, the palisade provided some protection against an enemy attack. At the center of every village was a large council house, known as a *msikamekwi*. Ranging in length from sixty to ninety feet, these windowless rectangular buildings were constructed of sturdy logs and had wide doorways. Here, the Shawnee gathered for religious and political activities. Warriors secluded themselves in the council house when they returned from battle. When at war with the Americans in the early nineteenth century, the Shawnee sometimes took shelter in the council house when their village was attacked.

Each family lived in its own lodge, or *wegiwa*, which was similar to Iroquois longhouses and the wigwams of the Sauk, Fox, and Kickapoo tribes. To construct a lodge, the Shawnee cut young trees, stripped the bark, and lashed the poles together to form a framework having vertical walls and a curved roof. For sheathing, they stripped large sheets of bark from elm or birch trees. The sheets were allowed to dry a little. Then while still pliable, they were laid over the structure. Rows of slender poles were laid over the bark, which was then tied to the frame. When bark was not easy

ade of saplings lashed together, the wegiwa frame was covered with layers of tree bark, which like shingles, readily shed the rain.

to strip from the trees, animal skins were used. There were no windows—only an opening in one end for a door. A hole was left in the roof for the smoke from the cooking fires that burned in a shallow pit in the middle of the dirt floor. The inside walls were lined with raised, wooden platforms that served as beds. Lodges were sometimes furnished with shelves, benches, and tables.

Each family's wegiwa was warmed by a fire kept burning in the center of the earthen floor.

In the fall, everyone abandoned the village and went on a long hunting expedition that lasted well into the winter. During these trips, they constructed small, temporary lodges. When they moved, they usually did not bother to transport these lodges, since they could readily find more building materials wherever they stopped next.

After they came into contact with the French and the English, many Shawnee began to build log cabins like those of the settlers. Later, when sawmills were established, board homes and furniture replaced the traditional lodges and cabins.

Government

The Shawnee were a patrilineal society, meaning that one's ancestry was traced on the father's side of the family. Men also tended to dominate matters of politics and war. Although men usually held positions of leadership, women who were related to leaders could become village chiefs. Women also served as advisors in matters of peace and war. For instance, women had the right to demand that a war party be halted, and a woman elder was called upon to determine the fate of captives—whether they would be tortured and killed or spared. Moreover, women managed all of the farming activities and ceremonies in the village. They took charge of the game brought into the settlement, and they managed their households. Women were highly regarded in general. For example, it was customary to avenge a murder by blood or payment of goods—and a woman who was killed commanded more than twice the price of a man.

Political activities were managed by either a war or peace organization. The Shawnee had war and peace chiefs at the tribal, clan, and division levels. The war chief protected the tribe from enemy attack and decided when the men would go to war. The peace chief handled the daily responsibilities of managing the tribe. Clan chiefs were responsible for rituals. Chiefs inherited their positions. War chiefs also had to prove themselves in battle as leaders and warriors. There was also a tribal council made of the chiefs and elderly men who were consulted for their wisdom, but only the chiefs could vote in these meetings. It is believed that each village also had its own council.

Chiefs dealt with problems that could not be resolved by individuals and families. When a murder occurred within the tribe, the victim's family was entitled to seek vengeance. A relative was allowed to kill the murderer, and the matter was considered settled. Instead of retaliating, the victim's family could also accept payment in wampum—nearly three times as much for a female as for a male. Chiefs seldom intervened in these matters, unless the murderer was a prominent individual. In these cases, the chief gathered the necessary amount of wampum. Theft was considered a serious crime that required a trial by the village council and punishment by public beating. If the thief continued to steal from others, he could be killed without fear of retaliation.

Society

The Shawnee were organized socially into five divisions known as septs, each of which was centered in a village. Each sept had its own purpose regarding politics, warfare, health, or religion. For example, the Pekowi (Piqua) division was responsible for religion while the Kishpoko (Kispokotha) took charge of warfare. The Mekoche (Spitotha) undertook matters of health and healing. The Thawikila (Hathawekela) and Chalaakaatha (Chillikothe) were responsible for governing the people, and chiefs came from one of these two divisions. Membership in the division was inherited through the father's family. As the Shawnee fought for their survival against the French, English, and Americans, this system of divisions broke down.

The Shawnee also came to be defined by the territories in which they lived and established villages. As the tribe shifted territory, the Shawnee groups fluctuated in number, size, and composition. Often separated by great distances, each group tended to be independent of the others. Eventually, the five septs and these territorial groups formed the basis for the three major branches recognized today: Eastern Shawnee, Loyal (Cherokee) Shawnee, and Absentee Shawnee.

Shawnee society was also organized into clans. Children were born into one of twelve clans based on the father's side of the family. At one time, there may have been as many as thirty-four clans, but many, such as the Loon, gradually disappeared. The twelve clans were the Snake, Turtle, Raccoon, Turkey, Deer, Bear, Wolf, Great Lynx, Horse (originally Elk), Turkey Buzzard, Owl, and Rabbit. Each

*S*hawnee society centered on the family and the clan even after the bands moved west of the Mississippi River.

clan controlled the names that could be given to its members. These names were believed to be related to certain traits. However, by the early 1800s, a child's name could belong to the clan of either parent or to even a different clan. Individuals were selected for political and ritual positions according to the qualities associated with their clan.

3. Lifeways

Shawnee women raised gourds in their gardens and crafted the dried shells into ladles and other household utensils.

"The people are presented with a way provided by the Creator that they may follow so that they will live in a satisfactory manner, if they adhere to the law which she devised. Certainly, the law was made up for all of those who are traveling in the direction intended for human beings. Thus do they earn the right to the earth."

—from the Shawnee Laws

Cycle of Life

Birth. When a woman was about to give birth, she secluded herself in a hut built some distance from the family's lodge. If the newborn was a boy, she and the infant remained there for ten days. If it was a girl, they stayed for twelve days. Then a naming ceremony was held. Elders often proposed several names, or the parents suggested a name based on a trait or behavior they had observed in their child. Names were chosen that would bring good fortune and skills to the child. Care was also taken to choose a name that no one else already had.

The mother carried her baby in her arms for about a month. Then it was bound in a cradleboard. The baby remained in the cradleboard most of the day, until it had grown strong enough to sit alone. The baby was then allowed to crawl around the lodge, after which the cradleboard was used less often, unless the family was traveling. The Shawnee toughened infants by briefly plunging them into cold water or snow every day for several months.

*S*hawnee parents, including this proud, young mother with her son, have always cherished their children.

Childhood. Although parents tended to be strict, children were seldom punished. They were encouraged to behave by a few words of praise or shame from a parent or elder. Children were taught to be honest and hardworking, but rules were not forced upon them. A child was expected ultimately to be the judge of his or her own behavior.

Girls learned from their mothers and the other women in the tribe how to gather wild foods and raise crops. They learned to care for children and undertook the household duties. They became skilled at making clothing and various handicrafts. Boys were taught to hunt and fight from their fathers and the other men in the tribe. When boys were about nine, they began special training for endurance and self-discipline. Fathers toughened their sons by requiring them to plunge into the cold water of a stream, often first breaking the ice to do so. Boys were also taught the key leadership roles that they would need as adults.

Although their parents encouraged high standards of conduct and responsibility, Shawnee children enjoyed many lively games, jokes, and good-natured pranks.

Coming-of-Age. As they approached puberty, both girls and boys embarked on vision quests in which they fasted and sought a vision that might foretell their futures. Their faces blackened with charcoal, they went away alone into the woods, where they fasted and prayed in hopes of finding a spirit helper. This spirit helper instructed the young person in a particular skill, such as healing, and promised to aid them in the future. The spirit helper often bestowed personal medicine or explained how the seeker could obtain this medicine that would ensure power and good fortune.

*A*fter a young woman learned all the household skills necessary to raise a family, she was considered ready to be married.

When they were about sixteen, young women were considered adults, ready to be married and start their own families. Young men were considered adults at sixteen, but they usually did not assume all the roles of manhood, including marriage, until they were eighteen and able to protect and provide for a family.

Marriage. Marriages were usually arranged, or at least consented to, by the parents of the couple, although young couples sometimes courted secretly. The marriage was based on an exchange of gifts. The man's mother offered the proposal along with a gift of animal skins and other suitable goods. She left the gifts at the home of the young woman, whose parents then conferred with each other. The acceptance of the gifts indicated that the young woman's parents agreed to the marriage. Her family divided the gifts among their female relatives and prepared a feast as a gift to the young man's family. Members of both families gathered for this joyous occasion and the couple was then considered married. The bride usually went to live with her husband's family. By the early 1800s, these practices had generally been abandoned and couples married by simply living together. Divorce became more common, and either a husband or a wife could casually leave the marriage.

Death. When a person died, members of another division or clan took care of the funeral. Only men buried Shawnee men, but both men and women helped to bury women. They dressed the corpse in fine clothes and applied body paint. Then they buried the body, usually with the head facing west. Circling the open grave, friends and family sprinkled tobacco over the body, asking that the deceased not look back or dwell upon those left behind. When the funeral party returned to the village, a great feast was held. Mourning lasted for twelve days, after which there was another feast. Payment was made to those who had arranged the funeral and the remaining property of the deceased was divided among the relatives. The mourners then resumed their normal daily routines. However, grieving spouses were not allowed to change their clothing or wear jewelry or paint for a year. At the end of this mourning period, relatives held a feast and the spouse could marry again. The death of a prominent person was commemorated a year later in a four-day ceremony known as the "turning dance." The special ceremony included feasts and dances and was followed by a distribution of gifts by relatives of the deceased.

Warfare

The Shawnee's enemies included the Iroquois, Chickasaw, Cherokee, and Catawba. From the late seventeenth century, they began to ally with the Lenape, and from the nineteenth century, they began to ally with the Cherokee. Since ancient times, they had been friends with the Creek.

The tribal council met and decided whether or not to wage war against their enemies. The war chief announced their decision, although it was reviewed by a peace chief who could halt the attack. If he or she agreed that the men should go to war, a tomahawk was painted red and taken to the other Shawnee villages as an invitation to join the war party. Warriors then gathered at the war chief's village to discuss their plans. After this meeting, they held a war dance, and then set out on their own from their villages. Each war party usually included a shaman who provided spiritual guidance and cared for the wounded. As they approached the enemy, the young men hunted twelve deer and everyone had a feast during which the leader made an inspirational speech. Then the warriors advanced and attacked the camp or village.

When returning from a raid, the leader sent a messenger ahead to inform the village chief. This chief in turn notified the women who began preparations for a great feast. As the warriors approached the village, they began their war cries. Rushing to meet them, boys and young men were allowed to beat any captives until everyone reached the council house. There the female elder thanked the warriors for their gifts of plunder and prisoners. Captives who had been painted black were to be killed unless she spared them as they entered the village. Other captives were given to poor families as slaves or adopted by families who had lost a member. A peace chief then offered a war song in the council house, where the warriors, stripping naked, danced until dawn. Each warrior struck a post as he boasted of his heroic deeds. The warriors remained secluded in the council house for four days, drinking herbal beverages and eating as little as possible, after which the feast was held.

Hunting and Fishing

The Shawnee hunted all year long. In the summer, they hunted deer and fished. However, for most of their hunting, they followed an annual cycle that began at the end of September and continued through the winter. Abandoning their villages, they ventured into the forest and set up winter camps in sheltered valleys. While elders and young children tended the camp, the vigorous men and women left in search of game. They hunted deer, elk, bear, buffalo, mountain lion, and turkey. The Shawnee were especially skilled at imitating animal calls and disguising themselves so that they could approach close enough to club their prey or shoot it with a bow and arrow. They

Moving silently through the woods, Shawnee men hunted many kinds of game animals for the meat, hides, and fur.

wasted no part of the animals. They ate the flesh, used the fat for cooking, made the skins into clothing, used the sinew for thread and bowstrings, and fashioned the bones, antlers, and horns into tools.

During January and February, the men concentrated on trapping beaver and other small fur-bearing game. Then, as the snows were melting in March, everyone returned to the village. By the early eighteenth century, the Shawnee began to focus on trapping animals whose pelts could be traded for European goods. They devoted so much time to trapping these animals that they were often not able to provide enough meat to sustain their families through the winters.

Gathering and Gardening

In the spring, after the Shawnee returned from the winter hunting camps, the women prepared the fields near their villages. In April, they planted the crops. Plots were owned by individual households and were grouped in one area, usually south of the village. Women planted together, but each woman tended her own crops. From early summer through autumn, they also gathered berries, roots, nuts, and fruits such as persimmons, wild cherries, and wild grapes. In early spring they tapped maple trees for their sweet sap, which they cooked down to a thick syrup, and in the summer they raided beehives for the stores of wild honey.

Women grew beans, squash, pumpkins, and sunflowers. A few Shawnee who lived in the south also planted sweet potatoes. However, their most important food was corn. They planted several kinds of corn, including a red corn, a dark blue corn, a soft white

*S*hawnee women grew an abundance of corn, beans, and squash in small fields situated near their homes.

corn, and a hard white corn, sometimes called glass corn. Corn was eaten fresh like sweet corn or dried for later use. The hard, dry kernels were soaked to make hominy, or pounded into coarse flour in a mortar and pestle. This flour was baked into breads.

A cornmeal bread known to the early settlers as "johnnycake" (also spelled jonnycake), may have derived its name from the term *Shawnee cake*. This bread was also called batter bread, battercake, corn cake, cornpone, hoecake, ashcake, and journey cake. Popular in New England, the South, and the Midwest, this bread was usually shaped into a flat cake, then baked or fried on a griddle. When Native Americans taught English colonists how to cook with cornmeal, they must have introduced them to this dense cornbread.

Johnnycake

Ingredients

1 cup cornmeal (preferably stone-ground)
1 teaspoon salt
1 teaspoon sugar (optional)
1 ¼ cups boiling water (or heated milk or buttermilk)
1 ½ tablespoons vegetable oil

Directions

Combine cornmeal, salt, and sugar. Stir in water until the mixture is smooth and thick. Drop by tablespoons onto a skillet or griddle coated with vegetable oil, and fry over medium heat for about five minutes until lightly browned. Turn and fry the other side for about five minutes. Makes 8 to 10 servings.

For a richer johnnycake, substitute milk or buttermilk heated in a double boiler for the water. For a lighter johnnycake, thin the batter with an additional half cup of milk or water.

Serve like pancakes with pats of butter and maple syrup.

The Shawnee stored corn by hanging bunches of the brightly colored ears high in the rafters of their houses.

Clothing and Jewelry

Shawnee women made all the clothing for their families from the hides of wild animals. They mostly used deerskins. They also used buffalo skins, until all the buffalo east of the Mississippi River had been eliminated by hunters. Preparing the hides was a laborious task that took from ten to twelve days. After the deer was skinned, the hide was stretched on a rack and dried. Then all the hair was scraped off with flint knives. The stiff rawhide was then soaked in hot water and hardwood ashes, which contain lye. Afterward, it was rubbed with a mixture of deer's brain, liver, and fat until it became soft and supple. The deerskin was allowed to dry, after which it was often smoked over a fire to give it a tan color.

Women sewed pieces of deerskin together to make breechcloths, shirts, and skirts. They also made moccasins with rawhide soles that people wore on journeys and during cold weather. In the summer, boys and men wore only a breechcloth, a strip of leather drawn between the legs and tied around the waist. Girls and women wore deerskin skirts. During the winter, both men and women added loose shirts and leggings. Girls and women also switched to longer skirts for greater warmth. When cold winds and snow swept through the forest, people wrapped themselves in buffalo robes or fur cloaks made of bear or moose skins.

The Shawnee adorned their clothing with dyed porcupine quills, feathers, and paints. Men wore headdresses made of animal fur and decorated with one or more feathers from a bird of prey, such as an eagle, hawk, or owl. When preparing for a ceremony or going to war, people often painted their faces and bodies. After they came into contact with European traders, the Shawnee began to acquire many new goods, notably glass beads. They sewed the glass beads onto their clothing to create elaborate decorations. They often wore silver pins, necklaces, and bracelets as jewelry. Men especially liked to wear silver nose rings and earrings.

When the Shawnee began to trade with the French and English, wool and linen cloth came to replace deerskin as the primary material

*L*ike these two women, the Shawnee often adopted European-style clothing but still wore their own ornate jewelry.

The Shawnee acquired beads to adorn their clothing and make jewelry.

for making garments. Solid-colored fabric and, later, calicos and prints, were especially popular. From this time onward, the Shawnee generally adopted fashions similar to those of the settlers, yet retained some of the traditional features of their dress.

Handicrafts

Shawnee artistry was expressed in baskets and other textiles, carved wood and stone objects, and pottery. Women twisted hemp into rope and made bags for carrying food and belongings. They wove dyed reeds and feathers into mats. They wove strips of wood into various kinds of baskets. They wove some baskets so tightly that they could hold water. Other baskets were woven with spaces left so

*W*omen were skilled at many handicrafts, including weaving baskets, which were most often used for storing foods.

that grain or meal could be sifted through them. These sieves were made with strips of wood fiber from the hackberry tree. To obtain the wood fiber, they cut down a hackberry tree and removed the bark. They next pounded the trunk until the thin layers of yearly growth separated and could be easily peeled.

Shawnee men carved wood into bowls, ladles, and spoons. From the knots of hardwood trees they cleverly carved particularly distinctive objects. In many Shawnee families today, carved spoons are cherished as heirlooms and are brought out at special ceremonies, such as the Bread Dances.

4. Beliefs

The Shawnee believed that one god
created the world and all the
creatures living there.

THE SHAWNEE BELIEVED IN A SINGLE GOD WHO HAD CREATED THE WORLD. Although there is evidence that the early Shawnee may have thought of this god as male, the tradition of a female creator, known as Our Grandmother, was firmly established by at least the early 1800s. The Shawnee believed that Our Grandmother created the earth and made people. When people grew old and died, she gathered them into a net and brought them to the sky.

During religious ceremonies the Shawnee wear regalia that recall their history as a people.

It was Our Grandmother who taught people how to provide food, clothing, and shelter for themselves. She instructed them in laws and rituals so they would know how to conduct themselves. After she had shared this knowledge, she left the earth and went to live in the sky. Our Grandmother also made a number of powerful spirits that served as witnesses or intermediaries between herself and people. The most sacred of these spirits were Tobacco, Fire, Water, and the Eagles. Other revered figures and objects were the thunderbirds, the four winds, and the sacred packs. Each tribal division had its own sacred pack, called a *meesawmi*. The sacred packs held revered objects that helped to bring victory in battle, assured bountiful harvests, and provided cures for the sick and injured. Only the most prominent men and women in the tribe knew what was in the meesawmi.

From Our Grandmother, the Shawnee received the twelve basic laws that govern their way of life and their relationship with nature. The first law described the origin and purpose of the laws, their benefits, and the consequences of not observing them. It also provided guidance in the relations between men and women and prescribed the practices to be followed during menstruation, pregnancy, and childbirth. The second law covered a broad range of obligations. Each of the remaining laws dealt with an animal—deer, bear, dog, birds, wolf, buffalo, raccoon, turtle, turkey, and crow. Each law described how the animal was to serve people and how it should be treated. The Shawnee were also served by shamans whose medical arts consisted of a blend of magic rituals and herbal knowledge.

Our Grandmother most strongly influenced group ceremonies, and had little function in the vision quests, sweat baths, and other spiritual activities of individuals. The Pekowi division was traditionally responsible for religious ceremonies. Both men and women purified themselves in sweat lodges. Huddled in the sweat lodge, they prayed to the spirits. They poured water over heated rocks to create steam. Then they left the intense heat of the sweat lodge, plunged into a numbingly cold river or stream, and returned to the sweat lodge.

Rites and Ceremonies

The Shawnee came together for seasonal religious ceremonies. At the Spring Bread Dance, people prayed for bountiful crops, and at the Fall Bread Dance, people gave thanks for the harvest and prayed that game be plentiful. These dances were organized by the women and honored them for the hard work they did gathering and farming. The Fall Bread Dance, in addition, honored men for their prowess as hunters. Each dance included a feast of meat prepared by twelve women from the game killed by twelve hunters. These twelve hunters were chosen for this honor for life, although they could be removed for misconduct. Before a dance, the chief called them together. The dance opened with a ball game played by a team of the twelve women against a team of the twelve men. The losing team had to gather firewood for the feast and the bonfires that would illuminate the night dancing. Everyone in the village gathered to receive the twelve hunters on the dawn of the third morning after they had embarked on their hunt. While the women prepared the game, the hunters danced to the

*T*his vivid painting by Ernest Spybuck depicts a ceremonial game held between men and women of the Absentee Shawnee in Oklahoma.

rhythm of drums and deer-hoof rattles. An elderly man known for his oratory prayed to Our Grandmother. There were more dances until late afternoon when everyone gathered for the feast. The evening passed with more dancing.

During the warm weather between the Bread Dances, the Shawnee held social dances and other religious ceremonies. Among these was the Green Corn Dance held in August when the first corn was harvested. For this ceremony, which lasted from four to twelve days, everyone brought large amounts of food to the council house. An elder made a speech expressing thanks and encouraging people to conduct themselves properly. All misconduct and injuries except murder were forgiven as people renewed themselves for the coming year.

Also held in August, the Men's Dance, or War Dance, was organized by the Kishpoko division in some Shawnee villages. At the Doll Dance, dancers wore carved wooden masks. The Shawnee held a special ceremony when the first wild fruits were gathered and at the end of the stickball season. They also prayed to Our Grandmother at naming rituals, funerals, and other special occasions.

Games

The Shawnee enjoyed stickball, many games of chance, and footraces. Boys played a kind of marbles with stones or peach pits whittled into a round shape. They also competed in a contest similar to the hoop-and-pole game that was popular with many native peoples. The hoop was made from a grapevine and webbed with strips of bark. As it was rolled, the members of one team shot at it with bows and arrows. If a boy struck the webbing with an arrow, he won the game. The boys on the opposite team then stuck their arrows in the ground, and the winner threw the hoop at the arrows. He could keep any arrows that he knocked down.

The ball game that opened the Spring Bread Dance was a kind of football or soccer. In this contest the men and the women competed against each other—the twelve hunters versus the twelve cooks. First, a sacred prayer hoop made of white oak was placed in the center of the floor in a lodge. The women entered the lodge, sat in a semicircle, and tied packets of seeds—corn, squash, pumpkin, beans, and others—to a pole to symbolize fertility. The women then left and the men entered to attach bits of deer, raccoon, and skunk fur and an eagle feather to the pole. The hoop was then hung in an elm tree and the men and the women competed in the game. Players used a buckskin ball, smaller than a modern football and stuffed with deer hair. Men had to kick this ball, while women could carry it. The game was lively and often rough with lots of pushing and shoving. Wooden pegs were stuck in the ground to keep score.

One week before the Fall Bread Dance, the adults played a ritual dice game by shaking six painted peach pits in a wooden bowl having steep sides and a flat bottom. The peach pits were sanded flat and painted blue on one side and red on the other. Either fifty or a hundred sticks were used as counters. The men and women faced each other, but only one man and one woman played at a time. Each player took a turn shaking the wooden bowl, which had been placed on a folded blanket. Points were scored in a complicated system based on the number of dice of one color that turned up. The competition continued until one side had scored the required number of points. As in the ball game, the losers had to haul the firewood.

Storytelling

Through stories the Shawnee maintained their traditions. In the evenings, as they sat around the flickering fire in their lodges, both young and old people listened to stories about the history and beliefs of the Shawnee. These stories helped them to learn about their past and define themselves as a people. Here is one story about mysterious spirits and their relations with people:

The Star Woman

There once lived a man named White Hawk, who lived alone, far from any other Shawnee people. He was such a skilled hunter that the rafters of his lodge groaned with the weight of dried meat.

One season, White Hawk went on a journey to the west, where the sun goes in the evening and where he usually hunted. He made camp and the next morning he walked onward, the rising sun at his back, farther than he had ever gone before. He came to a distant, treeless place over which a dazzling light suddenly appeared. Walking toward this light, he found himself in a wide prairie. In the middle of this prairie, he noticed a level place where the carpet of bluestem grass had been cleared and the soil packed down.

As White Hawk approached, he realized that the clearing was a field for playing stickball. He noticed small footprints of people like himself scattered over the field. Looking for a path that led to the people's village, White Hawk walked around the field. But he found no path. Hoping to solve this mystery, White Hawk hid in some oak trees near the field and waited.

He soon heard a whirring sound high in the air and glimpsed a black speck descending from the sky. As the object approached the ground, White Hawk realized that it was a large basket with twelve women sitting on the rim, swinging their feet to the rhythm of a song. These were the Star Women, also known as the Twelve Sisters, who played stickball on this field every day.

As the Star Women began their game, White Hawk observed them. All were quite beautiful, but he was especially attracted to one of them. She appeared to be the youngest and he instantly fell in love with her. He rushed toward her, startling the Star Women who quickly changed their song, called back their basket, and rose into the air.

White Hawk grieved over his loss as he walked back to his hunting camp. He burned with such love for the Star Woman that he returned to the field the next day. But first he killed an opossum, disguised himself in its pelt, and hid in the trees.

When the Star Women arrived and started their game, White Hawk waddled slowly like a possum toward them.

The Star Women ascended into the sky high above the treetops and far away from White Hawk.

"Look there," cried one sister. "That opossum is coming to join us. He wants to learn how to play stickball."

But the youngest and most beautiful sister remained wary. "We have never seen such creatures on the prairie," she said. "He might be dangerous."

The Star Women agreed and quickly ascended in their basket.

White Hawk was even more devastated by his second failure. He made his way back to camp, but he could not eat a mouthful and he could not sleep that night.

The next morning, he was determined and he made careful plans. He pulled up an old hollow stump and placed several mice inside. He lugged the stump to the playing field, where he changed himself into a mouse and jumped inside with the other small rodents.

When the Star Women returned and began to play stickball, the youngest and most beautiful sister noticed the stump. "There is something odd about that old stump!" she cried. "It was not there before."

"Oh no!" answered an older sister. "It's always been here. See, it's full of mice."

The older sister struck the old stump with her playing stick and a little mouse scampered out. The sisters beat the mouse with their sticks and killed it.

This satisfied the youngest and most beautiful sister and the game resumed. But she soon stopped, now even more alarmed about the stump. She urged her sisters to leave the field, but they only laughed at her. To reassure her, they again whacked the old stump and out raced another mouse—this time it was White Hawk.

The sisters chased the little mouse all over the field, but they could not get close enough to strike and kill it. Finally, the little mouse raced toward the youngest and most beautiful sister, the one he loved. As he approached her, he suddenly changed himself back into White Hawk and hugged her in his arms. Terrified, the other sisters fled back into the sky in their basket.

White Hawk thought, "I must tell her what kind of a man I am so she will not be afraid of me." Speaking softly to soothe her, he told her many fine stories about his life. He boasted about the abundance of game he had caught and assured her that she would be happy with him. He then told her that he would catch many raccoons for her.

Convinced that he would take care of her, Star Woman agreed to marry him and they lived together for several years. In time, they had a son. Deeply in love with Star Woman, White Hawk sought to please her in every way. Every day, he swept the clearing in front of their lodge and left their son to play there while he went hunting. One day, while he was away, Star Woman told the boy, who was then four years old, about her own life and how she had come to be married. She said that she wanted to return to the stars to visit his aunts and grandfather. The boy was unhappy until she told him that she intended to take him on this journey.

While White Hawk was away on hunting trips, Star Woman gathered wood splints from ash trees and worked to make a basket. When the basket was almost finished, she asked White Hawk to hunt as many raccoons as possible so that she could dry and preserve a large amount of meat for the winter.

White Hawk did as she asked and Star Woman stretched many raccoon pelts and packed many baskets with dried meat. White Hawk was again hunting when Star Woman put the meat and pelts in the basket and left with their son. She told the boy that they must fly to the playing field where they would find the trail to her home in the sky. She sang:

> The White Hawk
> I am going
> To leave him
> Now
> I am going.

Hunting nearby, White Hawk heard his wife singing. Then he saw his wife and son flying. He called to her, "Dear wife, please don't leave me without letting me shake the small hand of my son."

Ignoring him, Star Woman began to sing the song of her sisters. She and her son rose rapidly into the sky.

Overcome with grief, White Hawk collapsed and wept. Later, he rose and went back to camp, but thereafter he wandered like a man who had lost his soul. Unable to eat or sleep, he wasted away until he was little more than skin and bones. Every day, thoughts swirling in his head, he stumbled back to the playing field and prayed for the return of his wife and son.

After a long journey, Star Woman and her son arrived at her father's village. She lived there happily, but the boy missed his father. Star Woman tried to soothe him, but he became sick and forlorn.

Her father told Star Woman that she should bring White Hawk to their village in the stars. He told her that she should also return with every kind of useful game and fur-bearing animal.

Weeping by the playing field, White Hawk was over-joyed when he saw Star Woman and their son returning from the sky.

"My husband," she said, "your father-in-law sent me to visit you. I am to invite you to join us to live amid the stars. He ardently wishes to welcome you. And he wishes you to bring every kind of game and fur-bearing animal that we have on this land. He especially wants a raccoon of which I have always been so fond."

White Hawk happily agreed. Quickly regaining his strength, he hunted all the animals that he thought would make fine gifts for Star Woman's father. As he brought in game each day, Star Woman prepared the meat and furs. When they had all they needed, Star Woman, White Hawk, and their son placed small samples of the meat and fur in the basket and they ascended into the sky. After a long journey, they arrived at her father's village. White

Hawk noticed that the people there were very much like his own people, except they were all naked.

Star Woman's father was delighted to meet his son-in-law and together he and White Hawk took the samples of meat and furs from the basket. As Star Woman's father placed each sample on the ground, it suddenly grew into a large pile. He then called all the people together.

"See before you," he told them, "that my son-in-law has brought you gifts of meat, fur, and feathers from all the creatures on earth. With these, you will eat food and make clothes. Help yourselves."

The people were overjoyed as they rushed to gather the food and the clothing materials. But as they ate and dressed themselves, they changed into the animal whose flesh, fur, or feathers they had taken—into deer, bears, wolves, beavers, turkeys, and many others.

As for Star Woman, her son, and her father, they all became white hawks, which have long been revered by the Shawnee.

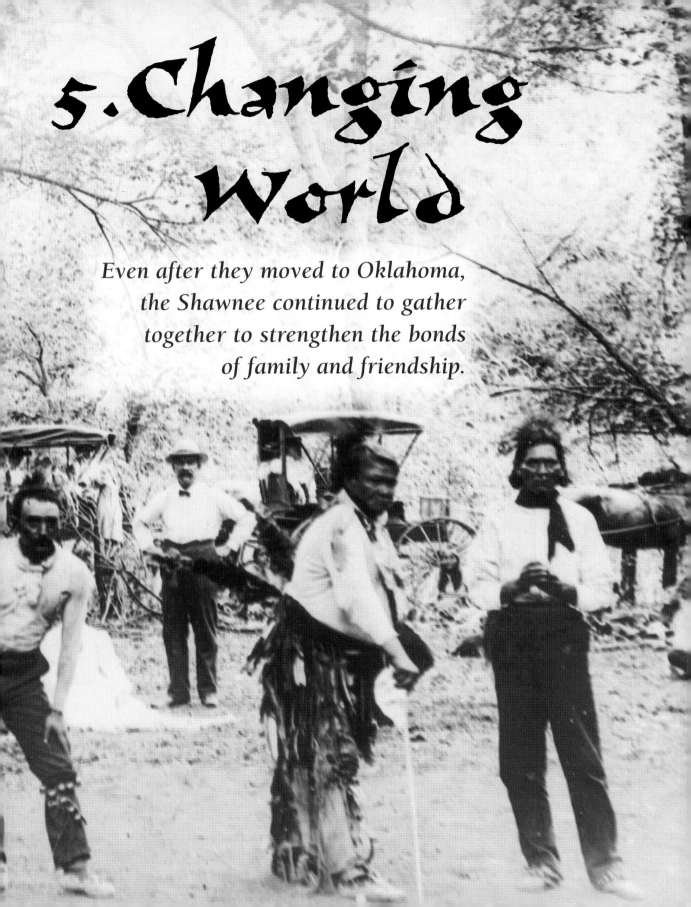

5. Changing World

Even after they moved to Oklahoma, the Shawnee continued to gather together to strengthen the bonds of family and friendship.

"The way, the only way to stop this evil is for the red man to unite in claiming a common and equal right in the land, as it was first, and should be now—for it was never divided, but belonged to all. No tribe has the right to sell, even to each other, much less to strangers. Sell a country! Why not sell the air, the great sea, as well as the earth? Did not the Great Spirit make them all for the use of his children?"
—Tecumseh in a speech to William Henry Harrison, governor of Indiana Territory, August 11, 1810

During the American Revolution, the Shawnee at first tried to remain neutral. To distance themselves from the conflict, many people moved west from the Scioto River to the headwaters of the Miami River and its tributaries. However, in 1777, some Shawnee warriors joined the Mingo in attacking American settlements on the frontier. The Shawnee allied themselves with the British in hopes that their rights to the land promulgated in the Proclamation Line of 1763 would be honored if the British won the war. However, the alliance was controversial among the Shawnee and nearly half of them refused to support either the British or the rebels. A number of Shawnee moved west of the Mississippi River into what is now Missouri. At the time, this territory was controlled by Spain.

The most experienced and defiant warriors remained and they wreaked havoc on the Americans, especially after the revered leader Cornstalk was betrayed. In 1777, Cornstalk journeyed with a peace party to Fort Randolph under a flag of truce to meet with soldiers. However, the soldiers took Cornstalk hostage, along with his son Elinipsico. After a settler was killed in a Shawnee raid, a mob stormed the jail and murdered Cornstalk, his son, and a Shawnee named Red Hawk. Cornstalk's death contributed to the Shawnee's continued hostility to settlers for the rest of the American Revolution and many years thereafter.

Warriors vigorously defended their territory, making it dangerous for all settlers. The Shawnee became especially known and feared because they frequently kidnapped and tortured homesteaders. Many of the captives were forced to run the gauntlet before they were slowly tortured and put to death. Others were not only spared, but also adopted into the tribe, often to replace a family member lost in battle. Perhaps the most famous captive, Daniel Boone, was held by the Shawnee for several months. A young man named Marmaduke Van Swearingen, who was adopted by Puckeshinwa, became the renowned warrior Blue Jacket. In the spring of 1782, Shawnee and Delaware warriors ambushed a force of five hundred colonial militiamen under William Crawford. The warriors routed the colonists, captured Crawford, and slowly tortured him to death. The Shawnee ravaged frontier homes and settlements in Kentucky, but their own villages were also repeatedly destroyed by American soldiers. The Shawnee were forced to move north to the Auglaize River.

After the war, the Shawnee, led by Blue Jacket and Puckeshinwa's son, a young chief named Tecumseh, continued to defy the Americans. These hostilities culminated in the uprising known as Little Turtle's War of 1790 to 1794. In 1791, Blue Jacket led a large force of warriors from several tribes in a surprise attack on Arthur St. Clair's troops along the Wabash River in Indiana. The

*F*orced to sign the Treaty of Greenville in 1795, the Shawnee lost their Ohio lands and had to move west of the Mississippi River.

warriors slaughtered St. Clair's forces, killing 630 and wounding 300 men. This was one of the greatest military victories in the history of native peoples in North America, prompting President George Washington to send a larger, more disciplined army to deal with the conflict. Led by General Anthony Wayne, this force defeated Blue Jacket and his allies in 1794 at the Battle of Fallen Timbers near present-day Toledo, Ohio. It was the most decisive engagement of Little Turtle's War.

After the Battle of Fallen Timbers, Wayne signed the Treaty of Greenville in 1795 with ninety-one chiefs representing twelve tribes. Of all the native people in the region, the Shawnee in Ohio lost the most land. Yet, driven to the point of starvation, they had no choice but to sign the treaty. In 1779 or 1780, the peaceful Shawnee migrated across the Mississippi River to Missouri to join tribal members already living there. Those who remained in Ohio eventually settled at Wapakoneta on the Auglaize River and at Hog Creek on the Ottawa River. Others joined with the Seneca who were then living in Lewiston, Ohio. A group led by Tecumseh moved to the Wabash River in Indiana Territory. In 1805, they moved to Greenville, Ohio, but returned to Indiana in 1808.

Tecumseh, a brilliant orator and military strategist, defied the treaty and dedicated his life to forging an alliance of all Native Americans to halt the encroachment of settlers on their ancestral lands. With the help of his brother Tenskwatawa, who came to be known as the Shawnee Prophet, he established his village near the Tippecanoe River in Indiana. Tenskwatawa encouraged native peoples to return to their traditions and

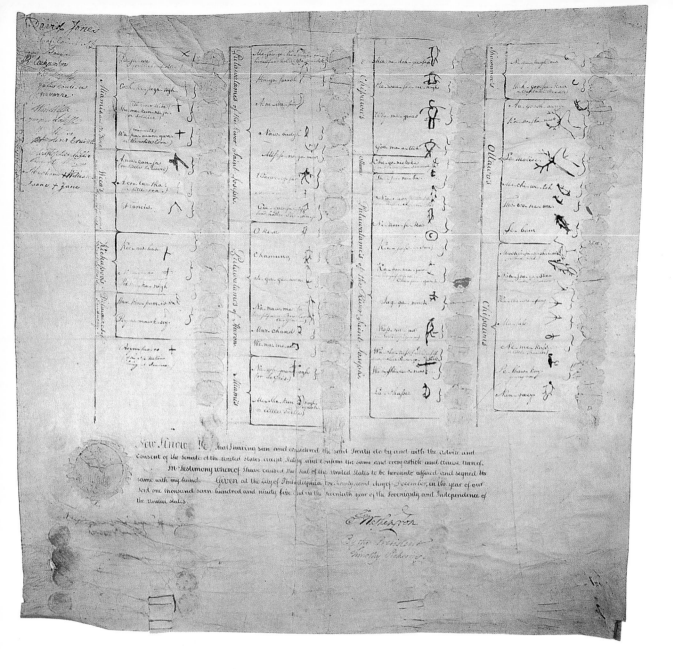

Shawnee signature marks are among those made by tribal leaders who signed the Treaty of Greenville.

reject all European influences, especially Christianity and alcohol. He also claimed to have powerful medicine that would help his brother Tecumseh and his warriors to resist the intruders. The two brothers envisioned a great confederacy of native nations stretching from Canada to the Gulf of Mexico. Unlike many Native American leaders, Tecumseh did not hate nonnatives. He insisted that prisoners of war be treated in a fair and humane manner. He studied European history and admired much of Western culture and technology. Yet he believed that no individual or tribe had the right to sell or give away any native land.

Tecumseh journeyed far and wide through the Midwest and the South to persuade warriors from other tribes to join his alliance. Through his eloquence, he convinced many warriors to unite in his pan-Indian cause, even those who had previously been loyal only to their own tribe. Curiously, although Tecumseh was a Shawnee war chief, many of his own people would not join his coalition. The Miami also remained neutral, but he convinced many others. Most of his followers came at first from the Delaware and then from the Kickapoo and the Potawatomi. The Sauk, Winnebago, and other tribes that lived farther west also strongly rallied around the charismatic leader.

In 1811, before the alliance had been completely established, Tenskwatawa unwisely attacked a military expedition led by William Henry Harrison, governor of Indiana Territory. Tenskwatawa's claims of invincibility became suspect, and after the warriors retreated, Harrison burned the village of Prophetstown. The alliance began to fall apart even before it had been completely formed. During the War of 1812, Tecumseh sided with the British

*T*he great chief Tecumseh allied with the British in the hope of driving the American settlers from Shawnee territory.

against the Americans. He hoped that the remainder of his alliance, united with the British army, would be able to vanquish the American forces. He became a prominent general in the British army and led several successful campaigns. But many warriors refused to take part in this war. Tecumseh was shot and killed in October 1813, during his forces' defeat at the Battle of the Thames in Ontario, Canada. Although Tecumseh came to be regarded as one of the greatest military leaders, at the time few Shawnee supported him and his brother. Most had already moved west to Missouri and those who remained in Ohio accepted the terms of the Treaty of Fort Greenville.

With the death of Tecumseh, all Shawnee resistance to westward expansion collapsed. The Ohio tribes, including the Shawnee, became refugees in their own land. They scattered and drifted in small bands into Missouri, Kansas, Arkansas, Oklahoma, and Texas. The peace faction of Shawnee that had left Ohio during the American Revolution settled near Cape Girardeau in southeast Missouri where they had been granted land by the Spanish government in 1793. A few years later, the Shawnee from the Creek confederacy, along with more migrants from Ohio, joined this division. Many of the newcomers belonged to the war faction and they came into conflict with the peace faction. In the early 1800s, most of the peace group moved away, drifting into Arkansas and Oklahoma, where they often lived among the Delaware and the Cherokee. Others were encouraged by the Spanish government to settle in Texas. But they were forced to leave and eventually moved to the Canadian River in central Oklahoma, where they joined members of the tribe who had been living there since 1836. These Shawnee were composed largely of the Thawikila, Kishpoko, and Pekowi divisions. In 1854, they came to be known as the Absentee Shawnee because they were not living on the Shawnee reservation in Kansas when it was allotted as plots of land to individual members. In 1872, the Absentee Shawnee were officially recognized as a separate division with rights to their own land in Oklahoma. A reservation was established, but soon thereafter most members accepted individual allotments and the land base was lost.

The Cherokee Shawnee trace their recent history to Missouri where they had lived since the 1790s. In 1825, however, the United States terminated their rights to the Missouri lands that had been granted by the Spanish government and established a reservation in Kansas. After passage of the Indian Removal Act of 1830, the Shawnee living in Missouri, who were known as the Black Bob band, and various remnants of the tribe from Ohio were relocated to a reservation in Kansas. The Black Bob band had opposed removal and its members fought with the Ohio Shawnee. Eventually, federal officials pressured them to move to Oklahoma, where the Black Bob band merged with the Absentee Shawnee living there. In 1869 the Ohio Shawnee joined the Cherokee Nation in eastern Oklahoma and became known as the Cherokee Shawnee.

Meanwhile another group of Shawnee from Ohio, that had been living with the Seneca, moved to a reservation in northeastern

Oklahoma. In 1867 they separated from their Seneca partners and from then on were known as the Eastern Shawnee. In 1937, when their separation from the Seneca was officially recognized, they organized formally as the Eastern Shawnee Tribe of Oklahoma. By 1900, most people had assimilated into nonnative society. However, through the early twentieth century so-called progressives and traditionalists continued to fight over preserving Shawnee language and culture.

From the American Revolution through the 1800s, the various splits and movements of the Shawnee were very complex. By the early twentieth century, the Shawnee had become the three distinct groups known today: the Absentee Shawnee, Loyal Shawnee, and Eastern Shawnee.

Shawnee Language

Shawnee belongs to the Algonquian language family, which was widespread in eastern North America. Shawnee is closely related to Cree, Ojibwa, Fox, Kickapoo, Menominee, Potawatomi, Delaware, and many other languages. All these languages are derived from a common ancestral language, often referred to as Proto-Algonquian, that was spoken by native peoples in the Great Lakes region about two thousand years ago. Some members of the three Shawnee divisions in Oklahoma still speak their traditional language. Efforts are being made to formally teach their children the language to keep it alive.

The following sample of words is based on the *Shawnee Language Dictionary* compiled by Bruce L. Pearson and published by the

Absentee Shawnee Tribe of Oklahoma in 1995. Shawnee is a complicated language, but the following key and examples should be helpful for approximating the pronunciation of the words.

Shawnee has four vowels pronounced as follows:

i	as in ma*ch*ine
e	as in gr*ea*t
a	as in *fa*ther
o	as in t*o*tal

Vowels are often lengthened, meaning the sound is held longer. These are indicated by double vowels, as in *wiikiwa*, in which the first vowel is held for twice as long.

Consonants are generally pronounced as in English, including *ch* as in *ch*ew, *th* as in wi*th*, and *sh* as in *sh*oe. Many Shawnee words are spoken with a glottal stop, or a catch-in-the-breath sound as in "Oh-oh." The glottal stop is represented by an apostrophe (').

A hyphen is sometimes used to indicate a part of the word to be emphasized, as well as singular and plural words. For example, *hileni-* means "man," and *hileni-ki* means "men."

Here are some everyday words used by many Shawnee:

Everyday Words

berry	miina
bread	takhwaan
cherry	waashimii
clothes	piitenikan
corn	taamin
dance ground	ta-menyeele-ki
hat	petakhoowe
house	wiikiwa
nut	pakaan
popcorn	pekwapwaana
shoe	ma'kithen

People

man	hileni
woman	kwee-wa
father	o'tha
mother	kya
brother	theetha
sister	mi'th
grandfather	me'shooma'tha
grandmother	ho'kom'tha

Parts of the Body

arm	n'kw
finger	lech-i
hand	lech-a
head	wiishiw
heart	the-i
knee	chiikwa
nose	chaal

Natural World

fire	shkote
month	kiisha'thwa
moon	tepe'ki
river	thiipi
road	meewi
star	halakwa
sun	kiisheki
tree	m'tekw-i
water	nepi
wilderness	piikwa

Seasons

autumn	tekwaaki
spring	meloo'kami
summer	pelaawi
winter	pepoo

Animals

bear	mkwa
bird	wishkilo'tha
deer	pshekthi
dog	wii'shii
fish	nameeetha
horse	m'sheewee
muskrat	hothashkwa
rabbit	petakine'thi
raccoon	ha'thepatii
skunk	shekaakwa
squirrel	hanikwa

6. New Ways

Today, the Shawnee are working to preserve their culture and improve their lives.

UNDER THE INDIAN REMOVAL ACT OF 1830, THE SHAWNEE WERE FORCED out of Ohio and Missouri. As different bands moved to Texas, Kansas, and Oklahoma, they united, then split again for various political reasons. Eventually, most of the Shawnee settled on reservation lands in Oklahoma, where they became three independent groups: the Absentee Shawnee who, with the largest number of native speakers, have been particularly active in preserving their traditional culture; the Cherokee Shawnee, who became known as the Loyal Shawnee when they supported the Union in the Civil War; and the Eastern Shawnee, who live in northeastern Oklahoma. All three were officially organized as a result of the Oklahoma Indian Welfare Act of 1936. They are recognized by the federal government from which they receive financial assistance.

Instead of rewarding the Loyal Shawnee for supporting the Union during the Civil War, in 1869 the U.S. government forced them to move from Kansas and settle among the Cherokee in Oklahoma. With about 8,000 members, the Loyal Shawnee are today the largest group of Shawnee. Most now live near White Oak, Oklahoma, although tribal members make their homes throughout the United States. When they were removed from Kansas, the Loyal Shawnee lost their legal status as a separate tribe, and their members are now officially carried on the tribal rolls of the Cherokee. The Loyal Shawnee still maintain their own membership rolls so that awards from any legal judgments can be fairly distributed among tribal members and their descendants. Since 1929, the Loyal Shawnee have won four court cases against

As they settled onto reservation lands in Oklahoma, the Shawnee struggled to make new lives for themselves and their children.

the United States that included monetary judgments. The tribe is governed by a business committee and a general council that determines membership eligibility.

The Absentee Shawnee settled near the Citizen Band Potawatomi Nation close to Shawnee, Oklahoma, in the central part of the state, where they had gained title to the land through an 1872 treaty with the United States. Under the Absentee Shawnee constitution, tribal affairs are managed by an executive committee headed by a governor. The Absentee Shawnee have their own police force and tribal court system. The tribe has about 2,000 members and a land base of about

12,000 acres. Income is generated from ranching, farming, royalties on oil and gas contracts, small businesses, bingo, and tax-free sales on the reservation.

The third Oklahoma tribe, the Eastern Shawnee, maintains tribal headquarters in West Seneca, Ottawa County, in northeastern Oklahoma near the Missouri border. After their removal in 1832, the Eastern Shawnee joined with the Seneca but were recognized as a separate tribe in an 1867 treaty. In 1937, the Eastern Shawnee adopted their own constitution and bylaws. They have their own tribal government and business enterprises, including a bingo casino, which employ a number of people. Facilities on their 800-acre reservation include tribal offices and a recreational park. The Eastern Shawnee provide much of their own health care, including a nutrition clinic for the elderly.

The United Remnant Band owns and operates Zane Shawnee Caverns on their traditional lands in Ohio.

*T*wice a year, the Shawnee host a powwow in Ohio to honor the traditions of their ancestors.

Today, about 12,000 Eastern Shawnee, Loyal Shawnee, and Absentee Shawnee make their home in Missouri, Oklahoma, and Kansas. Some Shawnee eluded removal in the 1830s and remained in the Ohio River valley, where they quietly followed traditional culture even as they attempted to blend with the farming communities of the region. In 1971, a number of these people formed the Shawnee Nation United Remnant Band (URB) and successfully applied for state recognition in 1980. The URB is now petitioning for federal recognition. This group of about 600 members has been working to buy portions of the land that once belonged to their ancestors. They have thus far acquired 117 acres near Urbana, Ohio, and 63 acres near Chillicothe, Ohio. One tract in what is called Shawandasse has been designated for use in powwows, religious ceremonies, and educational activities for young people. Another group, the Piqua Sect of Ohio Shawnee, is also seeking federal recognition, as is a Shawnee group in Indiana.

Each Shawnee group having state or federal recognition has its own chief. Tribal decisions are usually made by councils. Each group receives some government assistance and maintains rights to its own lands. Tribal leaders are striving for greater economic and political self-sufficiency for their people. The Shawnee in Oklahoma have generally thrived and have fared better economically than other tribes in the state. Yet the Shawnee are still struggling to maintain their language and traditions. The Loyal Shawnee have a cultural center and practice time-honored ceremonies, such as the Bread and Green Corn Dances, and a few people still speak the Shawnee language. Most Absentee Shawnee are now Christians, particularly Baptists and

A member of the United Remnant Band, this girl in dance regalia participates in the August powwow in central Ohio.

Quakers, yet they still participate in the traditional ceremonies. The Eastern Shawnee and the United Remnant Band also hold ceremonies and other activities to keep alive the spirit of their ancestors. Wherever they live, the Shawnee are striving to preserve the ways of their ancestors, even as they look forward to a brighter future for themselves and their children.

More about

the Shawnee

Timeline

1539 or 1540 The Shawnee encounter Spanish explorers in their territory in eastern North America.

1660s French and English explorers and traders enter the homelands of the Shawnee.

1682 French explorer René Robert Cavelier de La Salle explores the Great Lakes and the Mississippi River.

1754–1763 The Shawnee ally with the French against the British in the French and Indian Wars.

1763 The British prohibit colonists from settling west of the Appalachian Mountains. Shawnee join an uprising of Indian tribes against the British, led by Chief Pontiac of the Ottawa.

1768 Tecumseh is born in the village of Old Piqua on Mad River in present-day Ohio.

1774 In Lord Dunmore's War, Chief Cornstalk is defeated in the Battle of Point Pleasant. He is forced to sign a treaty recognizing the Ohio River as the southern boundary of Shawnee territory. Tecumseh's father, Puckeshinwa, is killed in this battle.

1775–1783 Americans fight the British and win independence in the American Revolution.

1790–1794 Shawnee warriors join Little Turtle's War and fight U.S. Army troops north of the Ohio River.

1794 American forces under General Anthony Wayne defeat Chief Blue Jacket and his warriors at the Battle of Fallen Timbers on the Maumee River.

1795 In the Treaty of Fort Greenville, the Shawnee and other native peoples surrender much of what is now Ohio, Michigan, and Indiana. The Northwest Territory is opened to American settlers.

1795–1813 Tecumseh tries to unite the Shawnee, Miami, Kickapoo, Creek, Cherokee, and other tribes to drive back American settlers.

1805 Tecumseh's brother Tenskwatawa becomes a powerful religious leader known as the Shawnee Prophet.

1808 Tecumseh and Tenskwatawa establish the village of Prophetstown. Tecumseh begins four years of travel among the tribes living between Missouri and Florida.

1810 Tecumseh and Tenskwatawa meet with Governor Harrison in Vincennes, Indiana.

1811 Tecumseh visits tribes in Michigan and the southeast to urge their warriors to join his confederacy. Harrison defeats Tenskwatawa's followers at the Battle of Tippecanoe and destroys Prophetstown. Tecumseh exiles his brother.

1812–1815 The Shawnee ally with the British against the United States in the War of 1812. Troops led by Tecumseh and British general Isaac Brock capture Detroit.

1813 Tecumseh is killed at the Battle of the Thames in Canada.

1830 Congress passes and President Andrew Jackson signs the Indian Removal Act. This law requires the Shawnee and other tribes to surrender their land in the east and move west of the Mississippi River.

1887 The Dawes Act eliminates reservations in Oklahoma and opens the land to nonnative settlers.

1901 Native Americans in Oklahoma are recognized as U.S. citizens.

1936 The Oklahoma Indian Welfare Act permits Native Americans in Oklahoma to establish tribal governments and receive federal economic benefits.

1975 The Indian Self-Determination and Education Assistance Act grants tribes greater control over programs previously managed by the U.S. government.

1980 The Shawnee Nation United Remnant Band (URB) is officially recognized by the State of Ohio. The band begins to buy back tribal lands in central Ohio.

Notable People

Thomas Wildcat Alford (1860–1938), educator and civic leader, was born along the Canadian River in Indian Territory. It is believed that his mother was the granddaughter of Tecumseh. Both of his Absentee Shawnee parents taught Alford the customs and beliefs of their people. At age twelve, Alford attended a mission school. He then won a scholarship to the Hampton Institute in Virginia, where he converted to Christianity.

When he returned home, Alford came into conflict with Shawnee traditionalists and he left to become a teacher. When he accepted a position as principal of a new federal school for Shawnee children, he settled permanently in Oklahoma. During the five years that he held this position, he also helped Shawnee adults adapt to changes in society. In 1893, he became chairman of the Shawnee business committee, and by advising Indians about their land rights he worked diligently to minimize the injustices of allotment. He traveled several times to Washington, D.C., to lobby on behalf of the Shawnee. He often drew upon his knowledge of traditions to convince others of the honor and dignity of the Shawnee way of life. He worked for the Bureau of Indian Affairs in the hopes that in that capacity he could influence policies to the benefit of Native Americans.

Alford and his wife Mary Grinnell had five children. Entitled *Civilization*, his biography, as told to Florence Drake, was published in 1936.

Big Jim (1834–1900), traditional leader, was born and raised on the Sabine Reservation in Texas. In 1872, he became chief of the Absentee Shawnee in Indian Territory. Big Jim fought to preserve the traditional culture of the Shawnee. He opposed farming in the belief that tilling the soil wounded the earth. He protested allotment in which, under the Dawes Act of 1887, reservations were divided into parcels of land to be granted to individuals. To avoid assimilation, Big Jim and a small group of followers moved to Mexico, where he died of smallpox.

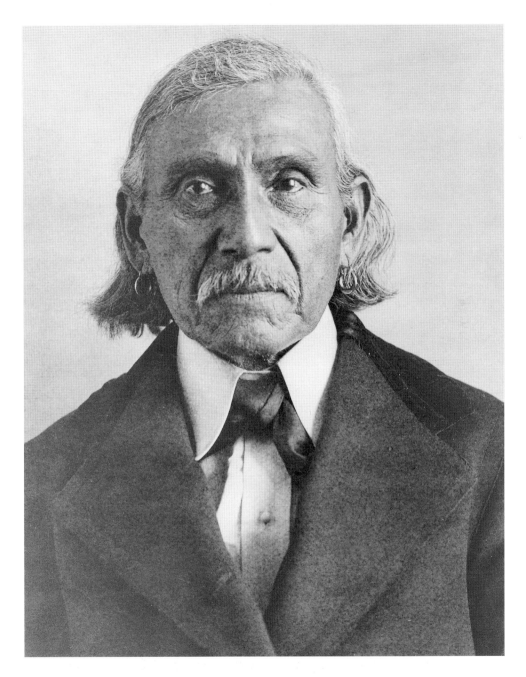

Big Jim

Blue Jacket

Blue Jacket (Weyapiersenwah; Wehyehpiherhsehnwah) (late 1740s or early 1750s–1805), chief and military leader, was adopted by Puckeshinwa. As a young man, he quickly rose to prominence and became a tribal leader. In 1774, Blue Jacket participated in Lord Dunmore's War, including the Battle of Point Pleasant. During the American Revolution, like many other Shawnee, he allied with the British. By the end of the war, Blue Jacket had settled along the Maumee River in Ohio, where he and Miami chief Little Turtle, Delaware chief Buckongahelas, and Shawnee leader Catahecassa established an alliance of tribes. During the 1780s and 1790s, these warriors vigorously resisted the encroachment of American settlers north of the Ohio River.

In Little Turtle's War of 1790 to 1794, native forces defeated an army led by General Josiah Harmar in 1790 and another led by Arthur St. Clair in 1791. However, Little Turtle believed that without English support native warriors could not ultimately prevail against the Americans. Blue Jacket then took command of the Indian forces in a desperate effort to stop the flood of settlers. On August 20, 1794, he led his warriors against troops led by Anthony Wayne in the Battle of Fallen Timbers. The warriors fell back in defeat, and Blue Jacket was forced to negotiate with the Americans. In 1795, representing the Shawnees, he signed the Treaty of Fort Greenville in which the Shawnee and other native peoples relinquished their lands in Ohio. It is believed that Blue Jacket was living near Detroit, Michigan, when he died in 1805.

Barney Furman Bush (1945–), poet and professor, is the firstborn in a large family that eventually grew to have sixteen children. Bush, of Shawnee and Cayuga ancestry, was raised in the Shawnee culture. His family lived as hunters and trappers in the rolling hills of southern Illinois.

Bush attended a one-room school for eight years. After his family was forced from their valley home by strip miners, he attended high school in another small town in southern Illinois. At age sixteen, he left home and traveled across the country to attend powwows and visit relatives. In Santa Fe, New Mexico, he studied jewelry making at the Institute of American Indian Arts and taught folklore courses there. In 1972, he earned a bachelor's degree in history and art from Fort Lewis College in Durango, Colorado.

For several years, he was active in the American Indian Movement (AIM) and then went to Oklahoma, where he helped to establish a Cheyenne school called the Institute of the Southern Plains. Afterward, he taught courses in Native American studies at the University of Wisconsin in Milwaukee. In 1971, he gave his first poetry reading at the Southwest Poetry Conference sponsored by Navajo Community College. In 1980, he earned a master's degree in fine arts and English at the University of Idaho. He has taught at Milwaukee Technical College, New Mexico Highlands University, and the Institute of the Southern Plains. He has also served as visiting writer for the State of North Carolina. To date, Bush has published four books of poetry: *Longhouse of the Blackberry Moon* (1975), *My Horse and a Jukebox* (1979), *Petroglyphs* (1982), and *Inherit the Blood* (1985).

Catahecassa (about 1740–1831), military leader, fought with the French during the French and Indian Wars (1754–1763), and helped to defeat General Edward Braddock's troops on their way to attack Fort Duquesne in 1755. Catahecassa also joined Pontiac's Rebellion against the British in 1763, and because of his heroics in battle, he became a principal chief of the Shawnee. He was a brilliant orator, as well as a great warrior.

In 1774, during Lord Dunmore's War, Catahecassa and his warriors helped to defeat Andrew Lewis and his troops at Point Pleasant. Along with Blue Jacket, he fought American troops in Little Turtle's War (1790–1794). He signed the Greenville Treaty of 1795 and other treaties effecting Shawnee territory north of the Ohio River. Thereafter, he sought peace and refused to join Tecumseh in his rebellion of 1809 to 1811. He died at Wapakoneta, Ohio.

Cornstalk (about 1720–1777), military leader, moved with his parents to Ohio in 1730. By the 1750s, he had become a principal chief of the Shawnee and a loyal ally of the French. In 1754, during the French and Indian Wars (1754–1763), he led attacks against the British. In support of Pontiac's Rebellion in 1763, he also raided settlers along the frontier of western Virginia. He became renowned as an orator, as well as a military strategist.

The Royal Proclamation of 1763 and later treaties established a boundary line for the territory of the Shawnee and other tribes from Lake Ontario to Florida. However, Lord Dunmore, the colonial governor of Virginia, awarded Shawnee lands west of the Appalachians to veterans of the French and Indian Wars. In response, the Shawnee attacked these settlers, killing them and taking captives. When Lord Dunmore organized a militia to put down the Shawnee, Cornstalk attacked a column led by Andrew Lewis at Point Pleasant in present-day West Virginia. Both sides suffered heavy casualties, and the warriors withdrew. Meanwhile, Lord Dunmore led his troops to the Shawnee village of Chillicothe, Ohio. There, Cornstalk faced by an overwhelming force, agreed to the terms of the Treaty of Camp Charlotte.

Thereafter, Cornstalk tried to maintain peaceful relations, but warriors continued their assaults. After journeying to Fort Randolph under a flag of truce, Cornstalk was imprisoned and murdered in jail by a band of militiamen. The killers were tried but acquitted. Cornstalk's death contributed to the Shawnee's continued hostility to settlers and to Little Turtle's War of 1790 to1794.

Cornstalk

Donald L. Fixico (1951–), history professor, was born in Oklahoma. Fixico is of Shawnee, Sauk and Fox, Creek, and Seminole heritage. Among the Creek and Seminole, the name "Fixico" means "Heartless in Battle." Fixico attended school near the town of Shawnee before his family moved to Oklahoma City, then Midwest City, and finally to Muskogee, where he graduated from high school. He attended Bacone Junior College, then transferred to the University of Oklahoma at Norman where he earned a bachelor's degree in history in 1974, a master's degree in 1976, and a doctorate in 1980. He taught in various colleges and universities and was a postdoctoral fellow at the University of California, Los Angeles, and the Newberry Library in Chicago before accepting a position as an associate professor at the University of Wisconsin at Milwaukee. He has written several books, including *Termination and Relocation: Federal Indian Policy, 1945–1960* (1986) and *Urban Indians* (1991). He also edited *An Anthology of Western Great Lakes Indian History* (1989).

High Horn (about 1775–1812), scout and civic leader, a nephew of Tecumseh, was born in a Shawnee village in Ohio. As a boy, he was captured by an American general in Kentucky who named him James Logan and raised him to adulthood. High Horn married a native woman who had also been captured and raised by American settlers. He and his wife made their home in the Shawnee village of Wapakoneta in Ohio. High Horn believed that the Shawnee and other Native Americans should live peacefully with the Americans, even as settlers encroached upon their ancestral lands. He opposed Tecumseh and his efforts to form a military alliance of tribes to resist westward expansion. During the War of 1812, High Horn supported the United States and served it as a scout and spy. While in the field with two companions, he was wounded in a British attack and died two days later.

Paxinos (active mid-1700s), military leader, who was part Delaware, became a chief of the Minisink band of Munsees, a division of the Delaware tribe, in the late 1600s. Around 1700, some of the Minisink, who lived in what is now northern New Jersey, joined with the Shawnee then living in Pennsylvania, and Paxinos became their most powerful leader. A shrewd negotiator and diplomat, Paxinos artfully played the forces of the British, French, and Iroquois Confederacy against each other. Colonists referred to him as King of the Shawnee. In 1757, Paxinos and other chiefs took part in negotiations with Indian superintendent William Johnson at Fort Johnson in New York. Later the same year, he attended a peace council at Easton, Pennsylvania. About this time, Paxinos and his family moved west to Ohio, where the Shawnee allied with the French against the British in the French and Indian Wars (1754–1763). Around 1758, not long after he had moved west, Paxinos died.

Ernest Spybuck (1883–1949), artist, was born and raised in Oklahoma and began drawing and painting as a small child. Although he never received any formal training, he was one of the first Native American artists of the twentieth century to paint in a narrative style. His subjects included horses, cowboys, ranches, and roundups, and Native American dances and religious ceremonies. He often depicted the changes in Native American cultural life in the early twentieth century as evidenced in the clothing, housing, and social life of the people around his home. He was fifty years old when he first traveled outside of Pottawatomie County, where he was born.

In 1910, Spybuck met M. R. Harrington of the National Museum of the American Indian (Heye Foundation) in Shawnee, Oklahoma. The museum commissioned him to make several paintings that vividly illustrated Native American ways of life. He received commissions for the Creek Council House and Museum in Okmulgee, Oklahoma, and the Oklahoma Historical Society in Oklahoma City. In 1937, he took part in the prestigious American Indian Exposition and Congress in Tulsa.

Tecumseh (about 1768–1813) was born in the village of Old Piqua not far from present-day Springfield, Ohio. He was the son of Puckeshinwa, a war chief, and Methoataske, who possibly had Creek and Cherokee ancestry. His brother Tenskwatawa may have been his twin, or he may have been ten years younger. When Tecumseh was still a boy, his father was killed at the Battle of Point Pleasant in Lord Dunmore's War of 1774. An older brother raised him, but that brother was killed during the American Revolution. Another brother was killed in Little Turtle's War (1790–1794). In this war, Tecumseh fought in the victories against generals Josiah Harmar and Arthur St. Clair and in the defeat by General Anthony Wayne in the Battle of Fallen Timbers. Tecumseh refused to sign the Greenville Treaty in 1795, which forced the tribes of the Old Northwest, including the Shawnee, to cede most of their vast territory.

In the early 1800s, Tecumseh, who was also a brilliant orator, began to urge all tribes to unite in defense of their lands. In 1805, after a religious experience, Tenskwatawa, who became known as the Shawnee Prophet, began to call for the rejection of Western ways, notably Christianity and alcohol, and the return of traditional beliefs and practices. In 1808, the brothers moved to Indian Territory and established the village of Tippecanoe, also known as Prophetstown, at the confluence of the Tippecanoe and Wabash Rivers. Here, people from different tribes could freely gather, away from settlers and soldiers. However, in a second treaty of Fort Wayne, signed in September 1809, William Henry Harrison, governor of Indiana Territory, forced the surrender of lands in the upper Wabash. In August, 1810, Tecumseh challenged the validity of this agreement.

Tecumseh envisioned a vast nation for all Native Americans, stretching from Canada to the Gulf of Mexico. To spread his message, he traveled as far east as New York, as far south as Florida, and as far west as Iowa. While he was away, Tenskwatawa, who believed that he had special powers, ambushed William Henry Harrison and his troops while they were camped outside Tippecanoe. Although surprised, Harrison with his larger

Tecumseh

force repelled the attack and burned the village of Tippecanoe to the ground. This battle proved that Tenskwatawa did not have special powers and triggered other attacks against settlers before Tecumseh had fully established his alliance. In this single battle, Tecumseh's rebellion came to an end, before it had a chance to get started.

During the War of 1812, Tecumseh sided with the British in hopes that they would help to return lands to the Shawnee and other tribes. As a brilliant military strategist, Tecumseh helped his friend General Isaac Brock take Detroit in August 1812. For his valor in the British victory at Maguaga, Tecumseh was made a brigadier general in charge of about two thousand warriors from the allied tribes. After a British naval defeat on Lake Erie in 1813, General Henry Proctor assumed command of the British troops and withdrew to Canada. Disheartened that lands were being abandoned by native peoples, Tecumseh argued against the retreat. He convinced Proctor to take a stand in Ontario against William Henry Harrison and his invading forces. As they readied for battle, Tecumseh had a premonition of his own death. That day he put on his buckskin clothing instead of his general's uniform. In the decisive American victory in the Battle of the Thames on October 5, 1813, the great Tecumseh was shot repeatedly and fell dead.

Kentucky militiamen skinned a body that they thought was Tecumseh, but warriors actually hid the remains of their famous leader. For years, rumors persisted that Tecumseh would someday return and fulfill his dream of building a powerful native nation in America.

Tenskwatawa (1775–1836), spiritual leader, may have been born in the village of Old Piqua near present-day Springfield, Ohio. He was the son of Puckeshinwa, a war chief, and Methoataske, who was most likely of Creek and Cherokee ancestry. His brother Tecumseh was either his twin or ten years older. Although ravaged by an addiction to alcohol, Tenskwatawa came to be influenced by the Shaker religion. In 1805, he lapsed into a deep trance, after which he claimed that he had journeyed to the spirit world and had received guidance from the Master of Life. Tenskwatawa

Tenskwatawa

urged his people to abandon Western ways, not only its clothing and tools but also its religion and alcohol, and return to traditional beliefs and practices. He urged the tribes to no longer fight each other but to unite against the settlers who were taking away their lands. He claimed that he had received special powers to cure illnesses and protect warriors against death in battle. After he predicted the total eclipse of the sun on June 16, 1806, many people became convinced that he was indeed the Shawnee Prophet. In 1808, Tenskwatawa and Tecumseh moved to Indiana and established the village of Tippecanoe. Tenskwatawa provided valuable support to his brother's efforts to forge a powerful military alliance of warriors from various tribes. When Governor William Henry Harrison of Indiana Territory moved on Tippecanoe, Tenskwatawa predicted that the Indians protected by his special powers would rout the governor's troops. Even though his brother was still away building his alliance, Tenskwatawa ordered a surprise attack. Caught off guard, Harrison's forces managed to quickly recover and defeat the retreating warriors. Harrison then marched on Tippecanoe and burned the village. The defeat on November 7, 1811, proved that Tenskwatawa had no special powers and led to the breakup of the alliance before it was fully established. The brothers became estranged, and Tenskwatawa moved to Canada.

Tenskwatawa played no role in the War of 1812. He remained in Canada until 1825, then returned to Ohio for about a year before he was forced to relocate with the other Shawnee west of the Mississippi River. He lived briefly in Missouri, then moved to Kansas. In 1832, George Catlin painted his portrait. He died in 1836, never having achieved his great dreams.

Glossary

Algonquian   Most widespread family of languages spoken in North America. Native American tribes speaking Algonquian languages include the Abenaki, Arapaho, Blackfoot, Cheyenne, Delaware, Fox, and Shawnee.

allotment   A government policy, starting in 1887, in which reservations were divided and parcels of land were distributed to individuals.

Bread Dance   An important Shawnee ceremony of thanksgiving, forgiveness, and purification, held in spring and autumn.

breechcloth   A cloth or skin worn between the legs and around the waist; also breechclout.

buckskin   The hide of a buck softened by tanning and usually having a sueded surface.

clan   Members of a large family group who trace their descent from a common ancestor.

confederacy   A political, military, or economic union of tribes or nations.

gauntlet   Double lines of people wielding weapons to strike a person who is forced to run between them.

Green Corn Dance   A major Shawnee celebration held each year when the first corn has ripened to give thanks for the harvest.

Indian Removal Act   An 1830 law that authorized the relocation of Native Americans living east of the Mississippi River to Indian Territory in present-day Oklahoma.

Indian Territory   A region in the south-central United States, including most of what is now Oklahoma, where the U.S. government relocated many Native American tribes.

meesawmi   A sacred pack of the Shawnee, holding objects needed for the tribe to prosper.

moccasins   Soft leather shoes often decorated with brightly colored beads.

msikamekwi   The large wooden council house that served as the village community center.

patrilineal   Tracing descent through the father's side of the family.

shaman   A religious leader responsible for the physical and spiritual well-being of the people in the village.

sweat lodge   A dome-shaped hut covered with bark or mats in which men and women purify themselves.

wegiwa   A dwelling made of wooden poles covered with tree bark or animal skins.

vision quest   A religious undertaking during which a young person leaves the village to fast in isolation and find his or her guardian spirit in a dream or vision.

Further Information

"Our Grandmother" is based on C. F. Voegelin's *The Shawnee Female Deity* (Yale University Publications in Anthropology, no. 10), 1936. "The Star Woman" is adapted from *Indian Tales of C. C. Trowbridge: Collected from Wyandots, Miamis, and Shawanoes*, published by Green Oak Press, Brighton, Michigan, in 1986.

Alford, Thomas Wildcat, and Florence Drake. *Civilization, and the Story of the Absentee Shawnees.* Norman: University of Oklahoma Press, 1979.

Antal, Sandy. *A Wampum Denied: Procter's War of 1812.* East Lansing, MI: Michigan State University Press, 1997.

Berton, Pierre. *The Death of Tecumseh.* Toronto: McClelland & Stewart, 1994.

Callander, Lee A., Earnest L. Spybuck, and Ruth Slivka. *Shawnee Home Life: The Paintings of Earnest Spybuck.* New York, NY: Museum of the American Indian, 1984.

Clark, Jerry E. *The Shawnee.* Lexington: University Press of Kentucky, 1993.

Clarke, Peter Dooyentate. *Origin and Traditional History of the Wyandotts, and Sketches of Other Indian Tribes of North America.* Toronto: Hunter, Rose, 1870.

Clifton, James A. *Star Woman and Other Shawnee Tales.* Lanham, MD: University Press of America, 1984.

Cowan, C. Wesley and Hirschfeld, Corson. *First Farmers of the Middle Ohio Valley: Fort Ancient Societies, A.D. 1000–1670.* Cincinnati, OH: Cincinnati Museum of Natural History, 1987.

Drake, Benjamin. *Life of Tecumseh and His Brother the Prophet: Historical Sketches of the Shawnee Indians.* Lewisburg, PA: Wennawoods Publishing, 1999.

Eckert, Allan W. *The Frontiersmen: A Narrative.* Ashland, KY: Jesse Stuart Foundation, 2001.

Eckert, Allan W. *A Sorrow in Our Heart: The Life of Tecumseh.* New York: Bantam, 1992.

Edmunds, R. David. *The Shawnee Prophet.* Lincoln, NE: University of Nebraska Press, 1983.

Edmunds, R. David. *Tecumseh and the Quest for Indian Leadership.* Boston: Little, Brown, 1984.

Encyclopedia of North American Indians. New York: Marshall Cavendish, 1997.

Green, Richard, Tony DeRegnaucourt, and Larry Hamilton. *Archaeology of Prophetstown, Greene Ville, Ohio, 1805–1808.* Arcanum, OH: Historic Archaeological Research, 1994.

Harvey, Henry. *History of the Shawnee Indians: From the Year 1681 to 1854, Inclusive.* Millwood, NY: Kraus, 1977.

Howard, James Henri. *Shawnee!: The Ceremonialism of a Native American Tribe and Its Cultural Background.* Athens, OH: Ohio University Press, 1981.

Johansen, Bruce E., and Donald A. Grinde Jr. *The Encyclopedia of Native American Biography.* New York: Henry Holt and Co., 1997.

Langer, Howard J. *American Indian Quotations.* Westport, CT: Greenwood Press, 1996.

Malinowski, Sharon, and Anna Sheets. *The Gale Encyclopedia of Native American Tribes.* Detroit: Gale Research, 1998.

Malinowski, Sharon. *Notable Native Americans.* New York: Gale Research, 1995.

Pearson, Bruce L. *Shawnee Language Dictionary.* Shawnee, OK and Columbia, SC: Absentee Shawnee Tribe of Oklahoma; Yorkshire Press, 1995.

Pritzker, Barry M. *Native Americans: an Encyclopedia of History, Culture, and Peoples.* Santa Barbara, CA: ABC-CLIO, 1998.

Sugden, John. *Blue Jacket: Warrior of the Shawnees.* Lincoln: University of Nebraska Press, 2000.

Sugden, John. *Tecumseh: A Life.* New York: Henry Holt and Co., 1998.

Sugden, John. *Tecumseh's Last Stand.* Norman: University of Oklahoma Press, 1985.

Thom, Dark Rain. *The Shawnee: Kohkumthena's Grandchildren.* Indianapolis, IN: Guild Press of Indiana, 1994.

Sturtevant, William C., ed. *Handbook of North American Indians.* Volume 15. *Northeast.* Washington, D.C.: Smithsonian Institution, 1978.

Trowbridge, C. C. *Shawnee Traditions.* New York: AMS Press, 1980.

Trowbridge, C. C. and C. E. Schorer. *Indian Tales of C.C. Trowbridge: Collected from Wyandots, Miamis, and Shawanoes.* Edited by C. E. Schorer. Brighton, MI: Green Oak Press, 1986.

Wheeler-Voegelin, Erminie. *Mortuary Customs of the Shawnee and Other Eastern Tribes.* New York: AMS Press, 1980.

Children's Books

Bierhorst, John. *The Ring in the Prairie: A Shawnee Legend.* New York: Dial Press, 1970.

Birchfield, D. L. *Tecumseh: Leader.* Parsippany, NJ: Modern Curriculum Press, 1994.

Connell, Kate. *These Lands Are Ours: Tecumseh's Fight for the Old Northwest.* Austin, TX: Raintree Steck-Vaughn, 1993.

Cwiklik, Robert and W. David Baird. *Tecumseh: Shawnee Rebel.* New York: Chelsea House Publishers, 1993.

Dolan, Terrance. *The Shawnee Indians.* New York: Chelsea Juniors, 1996.

Dominic, Gloria. *Red Hawk and the Sky Sisters: A Shawnee Legend.* Vero Beach, FL: Rourke, 1996.

Flanagan, Alice K. *Shawnee.* New York: Children's Press, 1998.

Fulkerson, Chuck. *The Shawnee.* Vero Beach, FL: Rourke Publications, 1992.

Hubbard-Brown, Janet. *The Shawnee.* New York: Chelsea House, 1995.

Immell, Myra H. and William H. Immell. *Tecumseh.* San Diego, CA: Lucent Books, 1997.

Kent, Zachary. *Tecumseh.* Chicago: Children's Press, 1992.

Landau, Elaine. *The Shawnee.* New York: Franklin Watts, 1997.

O'Neill, Laurie. *The Shawnees: People of the Eastern Woodlands.* Brookfield, CT: Millbrook Press, 1995.

Press, Petra. *The Shawnee.* Minneapolis, MN: Compass Point Books, 2002.

Spradlin, Michael P. *The Legend of Blue Jacket.* New York: HarperCollins Publishers, 2002.

Organizations

Absentee Shawnee Tribe
2025 S. Gordon Cooper Drive
Shawnee, OK 74801
Phone: (405) 275-4030
Fax: (405) 273-4534

Eastern Shawnee Tribe of Oklahoma
P.O. Box 350
Seneca, MO 64865
Phone: (918) 666-2435
Fax: (918) 666-3325

Loyal Shawnee Tribe of Oklahoma
P.O. Box 189
Miami, OK 74355
Phone: (918) 256-6914
Fax: (918) 456-6685

United Remnant Band
Shawnee Nation
P.O. Box 162
Dayton, OH 45401-0162

United Tribe of Shawnee Indians
P.O. Box 505
Shawnee Reserve 206
De Soto, KS 66018
Phone: (913) 583-3236

Zane Shawnee Caverns

7092 State Route 540

Bellefontaine, OH 43311

Phone: (937) 592-9592

Fax: (937) 592-4458

Web Sites

The Battle of Tippecanoe

http://www.rootsweb.com/~usgenweb/ky/tippecanoe/titlepage.html

Ohio's Indians Learning Links

http://www.oplin.lib.oh.us/products/PPF/ohioans/indians/links.html

Shawnee History

http://www.tolatsga.org/shaw.html

Ohio History Central: Shawnee Indians

http://www.ohiokids.org/ohc/history/h_indian/tribes/shawnee.html

The Shawnee Nation, United Remnant Band

http://shawneeurb.homestead.com/URB.html

Shawnee's Reservation

http://www.geocities.com/SouthBeach/Cove/8286/firstpg.html

United Tribe of Shawnee Indians

http://www.sunflower.org/~hdqrs/sindex1.htm

Zane Shawnee Caverns

http://www.homestead.com/zaneshawneecaverns/introduction.html

Index

Page numbers in **boldface** are illustrations.

Tippecanoe, 103, 112–114, 116
tobacco, 47, 61
tools and utensils, **40–41**, 50, 57
trade, 13, 19–21, 54, 102
traditionalists, 85, 92, 97, 104, 114–116
transportation, 13, 27–28
treaties, 22, **78**, 79, **80**, 94, 95, 102, 108, 112

uprisings, 20–21, 22, 77–79, 102
    See also Tecumseh

vengeance, 23, 35
villages, 13, 15, 32, 36
    See also rivers
vision quests, 44

war dance, 64
warfare, 13, 17–18, 19, 21–22, 23, 29, 32,
    35, 37, 47–48, 76–79
    See also battles; specific wars
War of 1812, 81–83, 110, 114, 116
Wayne, Anthony, 79, 102
weapons, 47, 49, 50
weather, 24
Web sites, 124
women, 35, 41, **43**, 44–46, **45**, 48, 50, 53,
    55, 56, 62, 65
    laws regarding, 61
writers, 110

Raymond Bial

HAS PUBLISHED MORE THAN THIRTY CRITICALLY ACCLAIMED BOOKS OF PHO-tographs for children and adults. His photo-essays for children include *Corn Belt Harvest, Amish Home, Frontier Home, Shaker Home, The Underground Railroad, Portrait of a Farm Family, With Needle and Thread: A Book About Quilts, Mist Over the Mountains: Appalachia and Its People, Cajun Home,* and *Where Lincoln Walked.*

He is currently immersed in writing *Lifeways,* a series of books about Native Americans. As with his other work, Bial's deep feeling for his subjects is evident in both the text and illustrations. He travels to tribal cultural centers, photographing homes, artifacts, and surroundings and learning firsthand about the national lifeways of these peoples.

A full-time library director at a small college in Champaign, Illinois, he lives with his wife and three children in nearby Urbana.

DATE			
CHILDREN'S DEPARTMENT			
INDIAN BOOKS			
7 DAYS ONLY			
NO RENEWALS			
			.